"was too young to remei came, seeking the 'brig killing the People. But Grandfather told stories of what it had been like before, when thousands of the People still hunted and fished, free from fear of the murderous firesticks. Ishi's own father had been killed by a firestick in a sweeping massacre which destroyed almost all of the Yahi nation. The seven remaining Yahi Indians —the boy Ishi among them—began a fugitive life. How Ishi and his tiny entourage lived and dwindled in 40 years of hiding is the inspiration for this sensitive biography, based on the author's scrupulous research. Our world discovered Ishi—or rather he it—in 1911, when he stumbled, exhausted and starving, into the mining town of Oroville, Calif. In middle age, he was the lone survivor of his tribe. Mrs. Kroeber's husband was one of the anthropologists who befriended Ishi. Now from all that is truly known of Ishi and of his nearly lost culture, Mrs. Kroeber has fashioned . . . a credible picture of a brave boy, a loyal son, a proud man; and, above all, a loving, gentle, dignified individual."

—The New York Times

ISHI
LAST OF HIS TRIBE

THEODORA KROEBER

*Text Illustrations
by Ruth Robbins*

BANTAM BOOKS · TORONTO · NEW YORK · LONDON

This low-priced Bantam Book
has been completely reset in a type face
designed for easy reading, and was printed
from new plates. It contains the complete
text of the original hard-cover edition.
NOT ONE WORD HAS BEEN OMITTED.

ISHI, LAST OF HIS TRIBE

*A Bantam Book / published by arrangement with
Parnassus Press*

PRINTING HISTORY

Parnassus edition published September 1964

2nd printing ...... January 1965	4th printing .... March 1970
3rd printing .... July 1966	5th printing .... May 1973

Bantam edition / September 1973

2nd printing .... March 1974	6th printing ...... January 1978
3rd printing .. November 1974	7th printing .. November 1978
4th printing .... March 1976	8th printing .. December 1978
5th printing .... February 1977	9th printing .... February 1980
10th printing .... July 1981	

ISBN 0-553-20508-0

Published simultaneously in the United States and Canada

Bantam Books are published by Bantam Books, Inc. Its trademark, consisting of the words "Bantam Books" and the por-
trayal of a bantam, is Registered in U.S. Patent and Trademark
Office and in other countries. Marca Registrada. Bantam
Books, Inc., 666 Fifth Avenue, New York, New York 10103.

PRINTED IN THE UNITED STATES OF AMERICA

19 18 17 16 15 14 13 12 11 10

"Many moons after . . . those living in distant worlds could read and know how the People spoke and who were their Gods and Heroes and what was their Way."

1

THE MOON SEASONS

MORNING mists, white and still, filled Yuna Canyon, clinging to boulders and bushes, and to the round, earth-covered houses in the village of Tuliyani. The fires in the houses were banked; no smoke came out the smokeholes.

In the men's house, three men and a boy lay sleeping. Each was rolled up in a rabbitskin blanket; only the brush of long black hair at one end of the roll made them look different from four bundles of alder tree logs. Nearby, in the family house, two women and a young girl were also sleeping, wrapped head to foot in rabbitskin.

The boy, Ishi, wakened. He inched himself free of the cocoon of rabbitskin, and without waking Elder Uncle or Grandfather or Timawi, went up the ladder post and out the smokehole. Dropping to the ground, he moved, ghost-quiet, past the house where his mother and grandmother and cousin were sleeping, and into the trees beyond the village.

Ishi did not take the long, meandering trail which led out of the canyon; he crawled on all fours under the wet bushes, then climbed a vertical wall of rock which was a shortcut to the top. From there, he followed the rim trail uphill, which brought him to Black Rock.

Black Rock stood three times the height of a man, smooth and shiny, alone and different. Holding with fingers and toes to the lichen growing on its slippery surface, Ishi climbed it. A shallow waterworn depression at the top made a seat from which he could see some of the rim trail and all around without being seen. This was Ishi's secret place. He said nothing to Elder Uncle or to Mother about coming to Black Rock.

They would worry and they have many worries already.

Tushi, Ishi's cousin, did not know about his

1

coming to Black Rock. *She is younger than I, and there are certain matters which it is not good to tell a girl.*

Only Timawi knew that Ishi came to Black Rock. *Timawi is older than I am and has his own secret place. This is as it should be with the Wanasi, the Young Hunters, of the village.*

When Ishi and Tushi were together, they talked of many things and laughed and Tushi asked many questions. Yesterday, she asked, "Who are the saldu?"

Ishi answered, "They are the whiteskin ones who hunt deer in our meadows and catch salmon in our creeks."

"Why don't they hunt and fish in their own meadows and creeks?"

"I believe they have none of their own; perhaps they were made to leave their own land."

"Why were they made to leave?"

"Little Cousin, I cannot say."

Mother does not wish me to say much about the saldu to Tushi. She says Tushi is too young to hear such talk.

Beyond Black Rock, the trail went across meadows, then up and up to the mountain, Waganupa. From Waganupa flowed two creeks, Yuna Creek to the north, Banya Creek to the south. These creeks cut canyons through the land, with ridges and hills and flats and meadows between. This was Ishi's world, the World of the Yahi People.

He liked to sit on Black Rock, as the God Jupka had sat on Waganupa in the Olden Days, watching the morning mists melt off. Bit by bit, he could see east and south and north and west; he could even see a piece of the distant Great Valley and the River Daha which looked to him like a milkweed rope lying in curves and bends on the valley floor.

Sun came up over Waganupa, melting the

2

last of the white mists. A flicker called from a tall pine tree, yagka yagka; a quail in the underbrush said sigaga sigaga; and there was the murmur of Yuna Creek at the bottom of the canyon. But it was for another sound Ishi was waiting. Soon he heard it, Whu–HOOH–huu.

Raising himself on his hands, he saw the Monster come in sight behind the River Daha, follow the river for a short way and go out of sight around a bend. So it had come with each rising and setting of Sun since Ishi could remember. It was black with a long, snakelike body. Smoke poured from its head and hung in the air behind it long after it was gone.

I used to be afraid of the Monster. I was sure it was coming up Yuna Canyon and into Tuliyani. But Mother said no, it belonged to the saldu and never left the river-valley. When I say to Tushi, "It calls from far, far away," she says, "It sounds lonesome."

Sometimes Ishi dreamed of the Monster. In his dream, he left the hills of home and went to the valley where he saw it close-up. He told no one of this dream.

Whether it is a Power Dream or a dream of no meaning, I do not know. Grandfather says a Power Dream is sent by a God or a Hero for a reason which may not be understood for many moons. Such a dream may one day give its owner power to cure a sickness or to become a great hunter, if he proves himself worthy.

I will prove myself worthy! My nose-ornament touches Grandfather's when we stand together. In another turning of the moons it will touch Elder Uncle's. This winter I will make a hunting bow and go to the high hills to fast and pray. I will draw my dream back to me!

A little lizard, called kaltsuna, sunned himself beside Ishi. Ishi smiled as he watched him puff his chest in and out and raise and lower

3

his body on short, crooked legs. "So—you know my secret, Little Brother," Ishi spoke to him. "You too like to see the Monster?"

Softly he brushed down the green head and scaly back with a blade of grass. Kaltsuna sat quiet, his eyes closed. "One night soon, North Wind will come from the mountain, bringing rain and snow into the canyon. You will find a dry place under a rock and we will stay close to our fires in Tuliyani until the New Year brings green clover and the spring salmon."

But I have to cut the juniper branch to make my bow! Ishi rubbed his empty stomach. *Su, su! I am hungry!*

ISHI started to slide down Black Rock just as the thod, thod of a horse, of two, three horses, reached his ears. Drving his elbows and heels against the rock, he pulled himself back to his hidden seat. The horses were coming down the trail which the saldu had made through the Yahi World, from Waganupa, along the ridge

4

between the canyons, down to the Great Valley. Now, one saldu, then another, came into Ishi's view. They were riding two of the horses, while a mountain deer was slung over the pack saddle of the third horse.

That is one of our big deer—it is from Upper Meadow—they must have spent the night there, and taken it at dawn.

The saldu stopped, dismounted and started on foot toward Black Rock. Ishi knew he could not be seen from the trail or from the brush— Timawi had made sure of that when Ishi first started coming here—but now he shrank tighter against the rock in fear. He must make no noise; he must see what it was the saldu did below him in the brush. Then, at a sudden thought, he put his hand over his mouth to keep any sound from going out on the air. He remembered a trap line he had set not many bow lengths from Black Rock!

Aii-ya! What will happen if they walk into my trap? Leaning far out over the edge of the rock, looking down through the leaves where he knew the saldu were, he spoke in a soft whisper:

May the roots of the manzanita catch your feet
    And throw you.
May the thorns of the chaparral tear your clothes
    And hold you.
May the poison oak snap against your faces
    So you do not see where you step!

One of the saldu slashed at the brush with a long curved knife while the other tried to turn over the hard-baked earth with a pick. A small berry bush came out by the roots and was thrown into the air, landing, unnoticed except by Ishi, in the top of a clump of manzanita. He could see his trap and tangled trapline there amongst the berry branches, and he sighed with relief.

The Brush Prayer is powerful. They will not find that trap; and never, never will I put another there. They look for the bright treasure, but they will find none at Black Rock.

The two saldu were sweating; their clothes kept catching and tearing on the thorns; the pick did little more than scratch the hard-baked ground; they found nothing. At last they gave up, returned to their horses, and, remounting, rode out of sight down the trail.

Ishi slid down Black Rock, untangled his trapline, and ran easily through the brush toward Tuliyani. *I shall not talk of this, not in the men's house, not in Mother's house. But I must tell it to Timawi and I shall do what he says.*

Only when he came in sight of home did he shake off his fright. The smell of woodsmoke and acorns hung in the air. He went to the firepit where Mother was making a basket of acorn mush. His stomach cramped with hunger. He sniffed the good smell and watched the mush boiling. Pukka pukka pukka the mush said as it puffed up in little mounds over the hot rocks in the basket and then burst with a poof! Pukka pukka.

Grandmother and Grandfather were seated beside Mother, and Elder Uncle and Timawi were on their way to the firepit from the wat-gurwa, the men's house. Ishi ran toward the creek, looking for Tushi. He met her coming up the creek trail with two baskets of fresh water. She smiled when she saw him.

"You went somewhere to look at the Monster, didn't you? I rolled my hair by myself, looking in the water."

6

Ishi nodded. "Like the loon bird. She looks in the water to straighten her necklace and admire herself."

Ishi took one of the baskets and they raced to Mother's firepit, trying not to spill any water. Mother, seeing them, said to Elder Uncle who had just sat down beside her, "They are alike, the young cousins."

"They are as brother and sister. You bring them up well, My Sister-in-law. Tehna-Ishi is now half-man, half-boy; he is a hunter and a dreamer; this can be read in the eyes."

"The son is like the father." Mother looked at her son. His hair was brushed and tied with a deerskin thong at the back of his neck; his deerskin sash was soft and fresh; he wore the matching ear and nose ornaments Grandfather had made for him.

Mother looked at Tushi and her heart hurt her that the Little One's parents were with the Ancestors, and that, because of the saldu, her life would be hard, or no life at all. Said Mother to Elder Uncle, "She is a dambusa one—pretty, gentle."

Said Elder Uncle, "Her cheeks are red like the toyon berry with all her running, trying to keep up with the boy, so much taller."

Tushi sat between Mother and Grandmother. To herself Mother said, "Grandmother has taught her to sit so the fringe of her skirt makes a circle of brown petals around her."

Mother filled small baskets of mush from the big cooking basket. She served Elder Uncle first because he was the Majapa, the Headman; then Grandfather, Grandmother, Timawi, Ishi and Tushi. Last of all, she filled her own basket. Ishi watched the wooden server in Mother's hand, back and forth from the round, large basket to the small acorn shaped ones.

He and the others waited while Elder Uncle

7

tested the mush for hotness and then dipped the two first fingers of his right hand into it, as a sign they might begin to eat. The first mouthful tasted so good to Ishi it almost hurt. He had not known he was cold until his fingers grew warm around the basket he held in his hand. Nor did he know how hungry he was until his stomach began to feel comfortable and full.

He wondered if there was food enough in the storehouses to keep the People of Tuliyani from hunger through the winter. He put his face down and smelled again the good smell of acorns: hot, a little bitter, like wet earth, like pine needles.

There was not much talk until the baskets had been refilled twice. In the silence, Ishi felt apart from the others. On Black Rock his thoughts had scattered from the top of Waganupa to the Monster; he must try to bring his thoughts home. He looked at his mother and at the others around her firepit.

Mother is smaller than she used to be. I am taller than she is, much taller. Her voice is soft like the big gray duck which comes only in the moons of the harvest. It says, sho, sho, sho. Grandmother told Tushi it was my father who gave Mother the name Wakara—Full Moon— because, he said, she moves in quietness as does the moon. When my father was here, I think she smiled more.

Grandmother laughs almost as much as Tushi. Her face and Granfather's are full of creases. It is good to have Old Ones at the firepit; they laugh and sing and tell stories and then we forget the saldu.

Elder Uncle decides where we may hunt and fish and what to do to keep the saldu from finding us. He does not give way to anger or to

8

wrong thoughts; and when he smiles I think I see my father.

Timawi is from the village of Bushki; he is the only one in Tuliyani who is sad. In Bushki, the hunters looked to the mountain, Waganupa, which is close to that village. My mother comes from Gahma or Banya Creek, and my father from Three Knolls, on Yuna Creek. They and their people looked to the water; they were salmon people. Timawi says some words differently from the way Mother says them. He changes from moon to moon. One moon he teaches me to shoot and jump; the next he sits in the dark of the watgurwa, and his thoughts, too, are dark. I wish Elder Uncle could help him to forget his sadness.

Tushi is smaller than I am. I have learned in the watgurwa that it is not good to make a hunting bow or to shoot deer with a girl. Tushi follows me wherever I go if Mother says she may. She laughs and her rolls of hair fall over her face and then down her back. Now she sits close to Mother and holds her basket as Mother does. She is serious when she stirs the mush in the big cooking basket with Mother's long wooden paddle.

Elder Uncle says I will sleep each night in the men's house with him and Timawi and Grandfather this winter. . . . He took me to sleep there for the first time when the salmon came up Yuna Creek. There have been thirteen turnings of the moons since I was born. Thirteen! It is time I cut the juniper for my hunting bow!

Elder Uncle put his mush basket on a rock and turned to Mother. "The winter moons will be with us soon. Timawi and I will put a fresh covering of earth over your house and the watgurwa today."

9

"That is good. Grandmother and I will make sure the basket lids are tight and everything where it will keep dry. . . . It is time, My Brother, to have the Feast of the Harvest."

"Yes, yes, I suppose so. . . ."

"There shall be the Feast! Are my son and his cousin to grow up like those Fat Ones with their full stomachs and short memories, knowing nothing of the Celebration of the Harvest?"

"You are right, My Brother's Wife," Elder Uncle answered quietly.

Mother means the People of the Valley who let the saldu take their land and gave no help to us when we fought them. . . . . .Elder Uncle is perhaps thinking of the great Feasts of the Olden Days.

The first meal of the day was over. Tushi and Grandmother were the basket washers and they liked to clean them before the sticky mush hardened. Side by side, they scrubbed and talked.

"Why do the Valley People have no Harvest Feast?"

"When the Valley People gave up their lands they also forgot much of the Way."

"The saldu hunt and fish. Why don't they have a Harvest Feast?"

Grandmother changed the subject. "The baskets are clean," she said after looking them over inside and out. "Set them on the rocks here to dry. No—in a line as when they are on Mother's shelf. Now come here while I fix your hair. You did not part it straight."

Tushi sat still while Grandmother unrolled her hair, parted it straight in the middle and re-rolled it, tying it with otterskin ties. "Now," she said, "that is better! About the saldu: they do not have a Harvest Feast because those who take the food of others without asking and without courtesy, do not give thanks for it.

10

"Back in the Olden Times, the Gods and Heroes held a First Feast and they told the Yahi People to make such a feast when the late harvest moon shines on the earth. It is a time of eating and singing and dancing. It is a good time. It reminds us of the Gods and the Way of Life they gave us.

"And now, you are to get your basket and digging stick and ask no more questions until after Sun has gone under the earth and climbed back up over the mountain once again."

TIMAWI and Ishi left the watgurwa the next morning by the light of a late harvest moon. As soon as they were in the brush, away from the village, Ishi told Timawi about the saldu of the day before.

Said Timawi, "You were right to say nothing of this to Elder Uncle. He might forbid your going to Black Rock. It is for us, the Wanasi, to keep a lookout for the enemy outside the canyon. We need not tell all we see or do so long as we do not show ourselves to the enemy, and so long as we do not find the enemy in places where Mother and Grandmother and Tushi might sometimes go."

Timawi shook his head over the trapline. "I did not know you trapped so close to the trail— set no traps or snares near a trail which the

11

saldu use. One snare would tell them that some of the People still live. They would search until they found us; they would destroy the last village and the last of the People as they destroyed the others."

Ishi listened to all Timawi said. *Elder Uncle and Grandfather say Timawi is a strong wanasi, a good hunter, and I want to be like him.*

Timawi and Ishi moved swiftly and silently through the brush. They were used to going together to look for treasure, to explore caves and to hunt small game far up and down the canyon. Today, they picked up the tracks of the saldu of the day before, following them to where a camp had been made at the edge of a meadow.

Said Timawi, "It is easy to track the enemy. The stiff leather in which they wrap their feet leaves tracks it would be hard to cover, and their four-footers have feet unlike those of brush animals." They searched through the ashes of the campfire and on the ground where the saldu had eaten and slept. There was no treasure, only the usual empty tin cans, and some scraps of rags and paper.

They went on to a stand of old juniper trees at the foot of the mountain, Waganupa. There Ishi examined each tree, choosing at last a branch for his new bow. It was straight and strong; the wood was not too young or too old, and it was the right thickness. Timawi, who had by now made several hunting bows, nodded when Ishi showed it to him. "Aiku tsub," it is good, he said.

Now they had to separate the limb from the tree. They took turns working and keeping a lookout for saldu, who might be hunting somewhere nearby. To get the branch off, they cut it a little, bent it a little, cut and rasped ever more deeply, bent it a little farther, over and over and over, until at last, with no tearing and no noise, it came cleanly off. Their only tools were stone and obsidian rasps and knives. They did not chop, which would have been quicker and easier. Grandfather had warned them, "Where there is the sound of chopping there is a two-footer. We know this; the saldu know this."

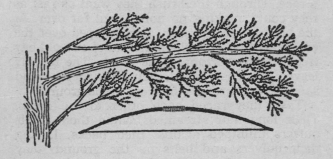

Sun was past the top of the sky and starting his downward journey before the branch was off. But, as Timawi said, "We did it with only such sounds as the rubbing and snapping of branches in the wind make."

To Ishi, the branch already looked like a bow. He laid it carefully on the ground, face-up as a bow is laid; and when they started home, he carried it in his quiver, face-up, as a bow is carried.

Said Ishi, "When I have my new hunting bow, we can go to Waganupa to hunt."

"Yes, and when there are two of us, I will teach you to hunt bear as I saw it done in Bushki. Also, we will think of a way to keep the enemy from taking our deer in Upper Meadow. . . . Tomorrow, Elder Uncle and I will take out our best bows. Perhaps we will go to the mountain to hunt."

"Then you must tell me each thing you do on that hunt. . . . Tomorrow Mother wishes me to go with Tushi to get many things which are needed for winter work in her house; Tushi cannot dig the heavy pine roots; and she cannot carry everything Mother and Grandmother want."

They were close to the canyon, "Suuuuh! A bear chases me!" This was Timawi's signal for a race. Through the brush they went as fast as they could, making no noise, bent far over. At the bluff above Tuliyani, they jumped over the edge, feet first, into the branches of two old bay trees which overtopped the brush. The heavily leaved branches broke their fall, so they slid safely down through the trees to the ground.

Then they raced each other to the creek. Their long hair streamed behind them; their quivers thumped against their backs. Laying their quivers and belts on the ground, they jumped into the creek—Timawi was first, but Ishi was only a bow's length behind him.

The next morning, the mush was eaten and the mush baskets cleaned and set in a straight line on a rock to dry. Tushi took two carrying baskets and her digging stick which Grandfather had made for her, the right length for her height. Ishi took scrapers, a flint knife, a heavy digging stick, and an old rabbitskin blanket to use as a wood carrier.

Together they went into the brush below Tuli-yani. By the time Sun reached the top of the Sky World, their baskets were almost full. They had dug pine roots to be used to make heavy storage baskets; cut hemp and milkweed for rope and strings; and found pine resin which Mother needed to fill the open spaces in cooking baskets to make them watertight. The four-footers and birds paid no attention to them as they worked and talked: they were part of the brush world.

Now they were hungry. Tushi had brought a

little bundle of food. They were also thirsty:
they would eat down by the creek. Ishi went
ahead to make sure there were no saldu there.
He found no footprints, no smell, no sound of
saldu. Tushi followed as soon as he gave a call
they used in the brush—plika plika plika—it
sounded like a woodpecker calling.

They stored their baskets and the blanket-
bundle of roots in the crotch of an old oak tree.
Then they lay on their stomachs, drinking,
drinking the melted snow water from Waganupa, from the Center of the World. They
held their breath and put their faces underwater. They felt good after the dry, thorny brush
and the hard work of digging.

While they ate salmon and acorn bread and
some of the berries Tushi had picked during
the morning, they buried their feet in the cool
mud of the creekbank and talked. A fallen alder
log reached from the bank where they sat
almost across the stream. Tushi begged Ishi to
tell her again about seeing two saldu on this
log.

"I was setting a quail snare," Ishi began,
"when I heard somebody coming. I climbed
into the bay tree there, just as two saldu came
around the bend of the creek. They were carrying firesticks and fishing poles. They sat down
here where we are, and chewed tobacco, spitting
all the time right into the creek. I knew then
why Grandfather says the saldu do not know
about keeping water clean and do not know how
to use the sacred tobacco.

"I was lying along a branch looking right
down at them. It is the closest I ever was to a
saldu."

"Tell me how they smelled!"

"Bad—the way a pile of old deerhides in the
storehouse smells. One of them leaned back
and turned his eyes up."

15

"What were his eyes like?"

"Like no-eyes, without color. But he could see; they must have a seeing magic we do not have."

"Tell me about their hair!"

"One had hair of no-color; the other, red hair, like the dye Mother makes. Over their faces grew much hair, and on their hands. These saldu cannot be truly men. Men do not have such hair, like a badger or a bear. They talked and spit for a long time and then No-Color started across the log. He slipped and fell into the creek and waved his arms and yelled. He cared most about getting his firestick full of mud and he sat a long time, trying to clean it. They crossed the log at last by holding a fishing pole between them."

"Like this! We are No-Color and Red Hair!" Tushi teetered out onto the slippery log and Ishi fell off into the creek, waving his arms and making his voice sound like a saldu voice.

They were now on the far side of the creek from home. By crawling on all fours under a matted growth of poison oak and manzanita up the steep canyon side, they reached the rim. There they stopped, looking and listening at the edge of the brush. Ishi wanted to go to Green Cave, but to get there they would have to cross an open, bare slope to the next ridge and then go down the ridge the distance of two long fish-lines to the cave.

Elder Uncle would say yes, it is all right for me to go. Mother would say no, Tushi must not go.

"You hide here," Ishi said. "I'll not be long."

Tushi's face puckered. "Why can't I go?"

"Mother and Elder Uncle would say no. It is not safe even to look into Green Cave."

"They why do you?"

"I won't look. I'll go quickly to get something

there outside the cave and come back, like Mole, under the ground." Ishi made the motions of digging with his front paws.

Tushi could not keep from laughing, thinking of Ishi traveling like Mole, pushing a pile of dirt ahead of him. She backed farther into the brush, becoming almost invisible even to Ishi. Leaves covered her face with patches of light and dark, and her arms and legs looked like manzanita branches.

Ishi wriggled along on his stomach, stopping to listen wherever a boulder gave him a little cover. In this way, he crossed the open slope and went down the ridge and out onto the lip of Green Cave. He did not look inside the cave, but kept his eyes turned away from the opening.

I do not like it here. The bones of many Yahi lie under the earth of Green Cave. I saw Elder Uncle and Grandfather and Timawi bury the bones.

It was a very long time to Tushi, waiting without moving or making any sound. At last she heard a closeby "Plika plika plika" and Ishi was back and pouring a pouchful of treasure into her hands: pieces of glass of different colors and something she had never seen before; white like dried clay on one side, and shiny with a blue flower pattern on the other side.

"I do not remember blue rockglass or brown." Tushi was holding the pieces up to see the sun through them. "Nor this white and blue rock which Sun does not shine through."

"It is to be found only where saldu have been. They bring it with them and throw it away."

"Why do they throw away treasure, dambusa treasure?"

"I understand nothing, Cousin, of why the saldu throw away this treasure. The rockglass will make fine arrowheads and spearpoints."

"But the flower-rocks will not." Tushi held up one of the white and blue pieces.

"I could make beads of them for you to wear with your shell necklace—if you like?"

Tushi looked down at her necklace, her rolls of hair falling forward and partly covering her face. "I would like that, Tehna-Ishi." To herself she said, "My cousin is sorry he could not take me to Green Cave." One by one she put the treasure pieces back into the pouch, making up a song to sing while she did this:

> White and blue
> Saldu treasure
> Says shu-shu-shu
> When I run!

"Sun is far to the west; we should start home," said Ishi when the pouch string was pulled tight.

"First we must go to Round Meadow to get Grandmother some sedge-grass. Maybe there will be time to play the Meadow Game too."

Round Meadow was across the creek from Tuliyani, an open space, level and round as the full moon, where five-finger ferns, sedge-grass, irises and marsh-marigolds grew. It was green there even when the hills were dry, and trees encircled it, shutting it in. It was a place of stillness, and Tushi and Ishi liked to go there.

They cut a bundle of sedge-grass, tying it with a long piece of the grass. Now their work was finished, and they played the Meadow Game.

They hid behind trees at the edge of the meadow. With a madrone leaf over his lips, Ishi made a thin squeal like that of a baby rabbit. Tushi called, "Sigaga, sigaga!" Ishi changed his squeal to the bleat of a fawn for its mother. Tushi said, "Kaug, kaug!" the way a crow calls.

There was a silence. Then again the meadow was filled with rabbit squeals and fawn bleats and quail and crow calls.

One and then another and another brown rabbit came from the brush, their noses wiggling and their white tuft-tails in the air. They hopped and waited. And hopped again. And waited. They were in the middle of the meadow and on their way to Ishi. A mother deer stepped from the trees into the open circle. The beating was repeated. Now it was answered, whoof whoof whoof.

Three deer and four more rabbits moved in the direction of the squeals and bleats. Several quail were hurrying toward Tushi, their topknots bobbing up and down. A crow answered her call from the top of a bay tree. A small red fox sat at the edge of the sedge-grass, his bush-tail waving, his nose going nuff nuff nuff! A bluejay, crying its harsh warning, flew low overhead, and a moment later, a fat brown bear walked from the trees into the open.

In a flash, Bear was alone in the meadow. Ishi and Tushi climbed the trees they had been hiding behind. Quail, rabbits, deer and the red fox melted into the brush. Bear circled once, twice, around the meadow, smelling and looking. Finding nothing, he left the meadow and went back into the brush. Ishi and Tushi slid down from their trees and ran for the creek crossing below Tuliyani.

Tushi stopped on a flat rock halfway across Yuna Creek. "Our baskets! Below the log! We forgot them!"

"They are safe there for the night. I will get them in the morning when Bear is sleeping," was Ishi's answer.

THE WATGURWA, Mother's house, and the storehouses were ready for winter: Timawi had finished putting a fresh covering of heavy earth over them. Grandmother watched him dampen the earth and smooth it. "The Bushki Hunter knows how to make houses like Flint Man's— they appear to be made of stone," she said with admiration.

Ishi stacked wood high behind the houses to be used when it would be too stormy to leave the canyon. Then he looked over his treasure in the watgurwa—here was work to be done during the snow moons! Besides the new bow which he had already begun to shape, he had a basketful of pieces of rockglass and stone and deerhorn, a bundle of skunk and squirrel and other small four-footer pelts, a roll of bird skins, and a basket of feathers. He was not yet allowed to hunt on Waganupa; his treasure came from the canyon, Round Meadow, and the nearby hills.

The storehouses were full. The largest baskets were taller than Tushi. They held white acorns and black, sweet ones and bitter; dried deer meat and smoked salmon. Smaller baskets were filled with nuts and seeds and dried berries. There were grasses and dyes and resin; and there were plants tied into bunches: roots for washing the hair, and other roots for making poultices; herbs for tea to cure headaches and stomachaches; and leaves of the sacred tobacco. Tushi put her face into them, making a hoom hoom song as she breathed in the fragrant-spicy smells.

"Aiku tsub, aiku tsub," it is good, Grandmother said over and over, as she looked into a basket, patted it and went on to another.

Timawi and Elder Uncle, leaving the others in Tuliyani, went to Upper Meadow to hunt. After five days, Ishi waited on Black Rock for them. He had not waited long when he heard the sounds of soft footfalls in the brush. But what he saw were the great spreading antlers of an elk!

A male elk leaves the meadow and leads his herd to the canyon! Ishi believed this for the time of an arrow's flight, as Timawi had hoped he would. Then he saw Elder Uncle and Timawi. Holding the heavy antlers on his own head, Timawi moved as an elk might move through the brush, and Ishi knew there would be fresh elk meat to eat and elk hide and horns to add to the treasure in the watgurwa.

While Elder Uncle and Timawi were away, Ishi and Grandfather had hunted each day in Round Meadow, and Mother and Grandmother laughed with pleasure when they saw what their hunting baskets held—ducks and geese! It was time for the Harvest Feast!

Before the feast, Timawi, Elder Uncle and Grandfather bathed and swam in Yuna Creek. For the Feastday, they wound their hair on top of their heads in ancient Yahi style. Grandmother, Mother and Tushi rolled their hair as usual, but it was freshly washed with the smooth root which is bitter to the taste but which makes hair clean and shining; and their fringed skirts of alderbark were new.

Ishi saw that Mother wore the sweetgrass bracelet which she usually kept in her treasure pouch. It was bound with the finest deer sinew and decorated with many tiny shell and rockglass pendants.

Father made the bracelet for Mother when she was a girl, before they were married. I wonder—is my mother happy today, and is that why she wears the bracelet?. . . . She looks happy.

Tushi wore her shell necklace with the blue flower beads from Green Cave. She stuck tufts of red woodpecker feathers in the mink strings which tied her hair today. Seedpod and shell pendants made her skirt say shu-shu-shu when she moved.

Tushi sees Timawi looking at her. He thinks she is a dambusa girl today. So do I think she is a dambusa girl today.

Sun shone warm, soft air blew through the canyon. The feast was eaten out of doors: fresh deer liver; stew of elk; duck and geese broiled on sticks and sprinkled with black salt which came from a nearby meadow; fresh grapes and hazelnuts.

Sun went under the edge of the earth; the harvest moon rose, full and bright; the feasters pulled feather capes around their shoulders and built up the fire. Grandfather smoked his stone pipe and said words of thanks to the streams for salmon, to the mountain Waganupa for deer, and to the hills and meadows for acorns and seeds.

Elder Uncle and Timawi and Ishi sang with Grandfather the songs learned in the watgurwa, and then they danced. They danced the Dance of the Hunt, and Ishi and Timawi danced the dance of the Wanasi. Then Grandmother and Mother and Tushi danced the Around-the-fire Dance of the women, dancing to the click of deer knuckle-bones which they held in their hands.

Ishi watched them as they danced. *Such are the women of the People. Grandmother, being old, does not circle the fire every time. But she stamps the earth as strongly as does Mother. And her voice is high, like a bird's. I think Mother looks tonight as she looked when my father named her Wakara. Tushi carries Grandmother's carved wand because she is a young girl. This is the first time she has been allowed to carry the wand. Never, never shall I forget this day's celebration of the Harvest!*

Mother and Elder Uncle, Grandfather and Grandmother sat by the fire. Tushi whirled round and round the dance circle, her eyes on the wand which she held high in one hand, singing a song to the click of the deer knuckle-bones:

> Shu-shu-shu I come
> White—Shell Woman
> Dambusa One
> From far away
> Shu—shu—shu I come!

Timawi and Ishi danced around the circle, outside Tushi and moving from west to east while she went east to west. Their dance was slower, earth-bound. The Wanasi must stamp the earth with a strong pumpf! And he must

23

bend his knees toward the earth pumpf, pumpf, pumpf!

The long nights and short days of the snow moons settled coldly over the Yahi World. Bear, snake, badger and owl were asleep in holes in the ground or in trees or under rocks. No deer went up or down the narrow trails to the creek.

It was cold, bitter cold. Winter was hard on the Old Ones. When they went outside they soon came back, shivering, to the fire. For Ishi and Timawi it was a good time. Outside, they wore deerskin moccasins with the fur inside, and feather or fur capes; and if the wind blew cold against their bare arms and legs, they raced each other till they were warm. Best of all, they had little fear of saldu in winter. Saldu did not often risk the narrow trails when they were frosty or ice-covered. Horses had slipped and carried their riders with them, rolling to the bottom of the canyon. And saldu did not usually walk long distances.

Inside Mother's house it was warm. Her house—the wowi—was built as were all Yahi family houses, with a single, round room dug into the ground to the depth of a grown man's hip. The room, about twelve footlengths long and wide, was large enough for Mother to cook by the center firepit, and for all seven of the people of Tuliyani to sit around the fire to eat or work. There was even room for all of them to sleep there as they sometimes did when it was very cold.

The inside walls were lined with alder bark and the floor covered with grass mats. Tushi, spreading fresh mats one day said, "Mother's house is a cooking basket—and the ladder, sticking up out of the smokehole, is a giant's mush paddle." It was tight as a cooking basket; North Wind was not welcome there nor did he find any way to enter.

Anyone coming down the ladder pole had to watch where he put his feet on the floor, stepping around whoever was sitting with a half-finished basket and dye and fern fronds, or with an animal pelt and awls and needles and sinew and thread spread out around him.

There were also Mother's cooking things to watch out for: a basket of water, another of acorn flour and another of stew; a grinding stone, a pile of cooking rocks, extra cooking baskets, firewood, and manzanita roots. The smaller baskets with seeds and herbs in them and the serving baskets were on shelves; the tongs and stirrers and paddles hung on the wall. Mother might be slowly burning some of the manzanita roots to charcoal. This meant the wanasi had brought her something fresh from their traps. When the coals were right, she would broil a

25

squirrel or a rabbit or several birds, to be eaten with acorn mush.

When Ishi came down the ladder pole, the warmth rose to meet him: warmth from the fire and reflected warmth from the low bark-covered walls. There were many smells in Mother's house in winter—the bite of smoke, the sharp spice of burning pine and baywood; hot resin; green and drying grass and bark; meat broth; still-warm bread; and the different smells from the baskets which sat in a neat circle on the upper house level: dried salmon and deer meat and bulbs and fruit; pelts and rugs and blankets. And there were the smells of tobacco and medicines and herbs which hung in bunches along the walls.

"There is the smell of snow outside," Ishi said, coming down the ladder pole one afternoon not long after the Harvest Feast. He lay down on the floor, looking through the smokehole which was also door and window. Tushi and Grandmother looked up from their sewing.

"I see North Wind is blowing leaves across the smokehole," said Grandmother.

"And there go the high-flying birds up to the Sky World!" Tushi climbed quickly up the pole to watch the ducks and geese overhead.

There were more birds, more leaves. When Elder Uncle and Timawi came in later, they brought the first snowflakes of the winter on their hair. In the darkening sky, the snowflakes raced faster and thicker past the opening over the warm fire in Mother's firepit.

It was during the snow moons Grandfather told the tales of Olden Times, and this night of the first snow, he began the tales with the story of the Creation of the World.

SAID GRANDFATHER, "Back in the Olden Days, the Great Gods, Jupka and Kaltsuna, were one day fishing in Outer Ocean. Jupka, throwing out a long line which sank deep into the water, fished up the uncreated world from the ocean floor. It floated on top of the water, flat and bare and empty, with no life of any sort upon it."

Ishi was no longer indoors by the fire; he too was fishing in Outer Ocean! The uncreated world floated before his eyes, while Grandfather's voice became the voices of the Gods.

"Said Jupka, 'I wish to make People, the First People. I shall call them Yahi.'

" 'That is all well enough,' Kaltsuna answered him, 'but the People cannot live on a land without streams or plants or animals!'

" 'True, true,' said Jupka, 'let us fill the world with all the People shall need.' "

Ishi looked into the fire without blinking his eyes. As Grandfather told what the two Gods did, he saw them step by step transform the uncreated world into the Yahi World.

"The mountain Waganupa grew at the earth's center, high and higher toward the Sky World, so high that snows covered its top. From the snowy top of Waganupa, the snows melted and flowed down the mountain in swift streams and falls, carrying rocks and boulders with them

27

and cutting the once flat land into canyons and ridges, hollows and caves.

"Pine forests, at first small seedlings, grew into tall trees on the mountain; acorns sprouted and became spreading oak trees; buckeyes and alders and madrones took root on canyon walls; manzanita and chapparal covered the hills. Grasses and clovers and many sun plants and shade plants bloomed on the canyon floors and in the meadows and over the ridges."

Said Grandfather in Kaltsuna's voice, "The Time of the Heroes and Gods, the First-Comers, has ended. But life must move upon the earth and under the water and in the air."

Again, looking into the fire, Ishi saw there the changing world Grandfather described. "A few Heroes went underground; two are said to live deep inside the mountain Waganupa. The others changed themselves into First-fish, First-birds or First-four-footers, each according to his nature. They became the Ancestors of our salmon; of the geese and ducks which fly between the earth and the Sky World; of bear and deer and all the other four-footers of the brush and meadows.

"When the Gods and Heroes had transformed themselves into creatures of air and water and brushland, Jupka and Kaltsuna sat on the top of Waganupa, looking down on the created world. 'It is finished.' This was Jupka speaking. And this Kaltsuna, 'It is time for you to make the People.' "

Grandfather took several sticks of buckeye of different lengths. Said Grandfather, "Jupka sat at the foot of Waganupa where he cut straight sticks of buckeye like these in my hand. He placed one stick—so—laying it east and west on the ground; blew smoke over it—so—from his stone pipe; and said to the stick, 'You are a

28

Yahi! You are man, hisi, the first of the People.'"

Ishi, who was lying on the floor beside the stick, now stood up, and, dancing around the fire, said in the words of the story, "So be it, O Great One."

Said Grandfather, "Jupka then placed a shorter stick on the ground, blew smoke over it, and said as before, 'You are a Yahi! You are marimi, woman, the first Yahi woman of the People.'"

Tushi, who was lying on the floor beside the stick, now stood up and, dancing around the fire, said in the words of the story, "So be it, O Great One."

Said Grandfather, "Jupka then placed two sticks side by side on the ground—so—blew smoke over them—so—and said, 'You are a boy! You are a girl! After you, all children will have a father and a mother. Thus, there will always be children.'"

Ishi and Tushi together danced around the fire saying, "So be it, O Great One."

"Jupka cut more and more buckeye sticks. He did not look up from his work until Sun was low in the west. By then, there were people in the canyons and in the meadows and on the hills and along the streams.

"Kaltsuna taught these first people to flake arrowheads, to make bows and harpoons, and to build houses. From him they learned to hunt and fish, to make fire, to cook, and many things besides. Said Kaltsuna to them day after day, 'Do this and this and this as I show you, and teach those who come after you to do the same.'

"Jupka taught the first people the meaning of the moons and seasons and what work and prayers and songs and dances belonged to each moon. He taught also something of the nature

29

of men and of women; and the rules belonging to the wowi and to the watgurwa. From Jupka they learned about death and the land of the Dead, and all matters which had to do with the Yahi Way. Said Jupka, 'Listen and remember all I tell and teach you now. In your turn, teach these things to your children and your grandchildren. Then, in the time to come, the People will always live in warm houses; their baskets will be full of salmon and deer; there will be peace within the watgurwa and the village, and between neighbors up and down the streams, and with the creatures of air and water and brush. The People will not forget their Gods and Heroes nor their teachings. In the moons to come it will be as it is now.'

"Jupka's work and Kaltsuna's was finished; the time had come for them, too, to transform themselves, leaving the World to the Yahi People."

Ishi and Tushi covered themselves with fur capes. Slowly, slowly, like a sleepy lizard, Ishi freed his head, then one arm, the other arm, and his legs. Barely moving, he crawled on all fours, his arms bent out at the elbows. He flicked his tongue out, in, out, in, and spoke, saying, "I, Kaltsuna, Maker of Arrows, choose to become a little rock lizard. My hide will remind the People of flint, gray flint on top, blue and yellow and white flint underneath. I will sun where the People sun and they will stroke me sometimes with a soft blade of grass."

Tushi slowly, slowly went round and round inside her cape, working, working to free herself. First her eyes came into view. Then with a pull, she seemed to tear her way out of a cocoon. She sat waving her arms, only a small motion at first, and then more and more freely in the movements of a butterfly drying itself and unfolding its wings.

"I, Jupka," she said, "choose to become a many-colored butterfly. The women will weave the pattern of my wings into their finest baskets. And when I flutter over the hillsides in the time of green clover and the New Year, I will remind the People that the world is dambusa and its Way a good Way."

31

EACH NIGHT Elder Uncle took Ishi to sleep in
the watgurwa with him and Timawi and Grandfather. Mother said, "You are awake over there
sometimes until the moon goes down below the
edge of the earth. The Young One should not
be awake all night."

Elder Uncle smiled. "The day is as good as
the night for sleep, My Younger Brother's Wife.
A man must learn to sleep with his eyes closed
against Sun—or to stay awake for as long as two
or three or four Sun journeys."

Mother shook her head, but she said nothing
more—Elder Uncle was the Majapa. As he
started up the ladder pole, she put an extra fur
rug over his arm. "For Grandfather," she said.

Ishi heard what Mother said and what Elder
Uncle answered. He followed quickly after Elder
Uncle. *I am sorry not to look at the Star People
through the smokehole with Tushi, and hear
Grandmother tell of how they came to leave
the earth and go to the Sky World. But—I shall
make the hunting bow during these snow
moons. The Young Hunter sleeps in the watgurwa where the talk goes on till dawn—the
talk of men.*

In the watgurwa, Ishi took his first sweatbath.
With his firedrill, Elder Uncle made new fire in
the firepit. Into the hot ashes of this fire, he and
Grandfather put waterworn stones which they
lifted with fire-hardened tongs. The rocks became so hot they changed color; waves of heat
filled the watgurwa until it felt like a firepit.
The three men and Ishi lay flat on the floor,
face-down. Elder Uncle said a prayer, and then

there was silence. The heat entered their bodies; it went all through them. Their hair was wet with sweat and the sweat dripped and darkened the floor where they lay still.

The watgurwa sweatbath brings to the mind forgetfulness and to the body unmovingness. In this heat there are no dreams. All is hotness and mist and nothingness. This is how it must have been when the new world floated on Outer Ocean.

After a long time, Elder Uncle made a sign and Ishi and the three men ran to the creek, going into water over their heads. After swimming back and forth across the creek, they returned, running, to the watgurwa. And there, Elder Uncle smoked a pipeful of the sacred tobacco and said an ending prayer.

In the water, there was only coldness. Running, I suddenly saw the world again. Now, I could run all day, I could climb the steep canyon wall. I feel power growing in me, I could hunt and catch many deer.

Ishi learned to stay awake. Adding night to night, he was able to spend five nights in song and prayer; and he learned to go without eating as a hunter must do if he is to bring deer to him.

Said Elder Uncle, "You learn quickly and well, Younger Brother's Son. You will soon be ready to go to the hills alone, to fast and pray there. And the Heroes may send you a Dream."

There were nights of good talk in the watgurwa, talk of hunting and fishing; and nights of talk of the saldu. One windless night snowflakes drifted down the smokehole, exploding with a zzzzzzs! when they reached the flames. Grandfather climbed the house pole to look out at the deepening drifts.

"This is snow such as fell when the saldu first came," he said, coming back to the fire.

33

Ishi touched his half-finished bow. *If no Older One speaks, the Youngest may do so at the watgurwa fire.* "Grandfather," said Ishi, after some moments of silence, "Grandmother says the saldu came out of the inside of Waganupa. But then she laughs. . . . ."

Grandfather gumbled, "It is better the wanasi sleeps here, away from the half-truths of the Old Woman. Glue another layer of backing to your bow and I will tell you how they came."

Ishi set a small basket of fish glue on a rock close to the fire to soften. Beside him were many pieces of deer sinew which he had chewed and scraped into thin strips to back his bow.

"It was a winter like this," Grandfather said. "It snowed and snowed, although it was the time of the New Year. One day, the People at Bushki, Timawi's village, sent a lookout to tell us at Three Knolls Village that fifteen or twenty saldu —men-like beings with pale skin and eyes— had come out of the desert which begins at the far edge of the Eastern Meadows of Waganupa and extends no one knows how far.

"The strangers came around the base of Waganupa and across Upper Meadow to the ridge trail where we could see them. We were about to send a lookout ahead to warn the people below us, but the saldu turned away from the ridge and took the steep trail leading into our own village.

"The women and children who were outside ran back into their houses and put out the fires there. To the saldu the village appeared to be deserted, except for your Elder Uncle, your father, the other wanasi, and me. And we were busy laying a trapline down one of the paths of the village.

"Remember, we had never seen a horse, nor any four-footer with a rider or a pack on his

34

back. But we had little time to look at them now. The saldu rode into the middle of the village; their horses reared and the riders shouted. One horse shied at a water basket and knocked over a drying frame. Another stepped into an outdoor firepit full of snow, throwing his rider, who hit the side of a house and went headfirst into a snowdrift.

"These were not men as we knew men. I was sure they were dawana, crazy, and that they had been driven from their own homes because of some wrong acts or thoughts. Why else would they come among strangers, and come in this way?

"One of them was in the lead and seemed to be their Headman. He started to get off his horse, but his foot caught in something which hung from his belt. We went closer to see what it was . . . . ." Grandfather's face drew in with pain and disgust. "His foot was caught in the scalp of a woman of the People! Her long black hair was still rolled and tied with otter fur ties like Tushi's. We saw that others of these saldu also wore scalps at their belts. Then I was sure they were demons.

"They understood no word of the Tongue, but we made out what the Headman wanted. He showed us a pouchful of the bright dust which is in our creeks. For what purpose the saldu want this dust I do not know. It is without value unless they use it in their magic.

"I thought—if it is this dust they wish, I will direct their feet to the south where there is much more in the streams than here, for I surely did not want these dawana ones near my People. Taking a stick, I marked in the snow the three knolls above and pointed to them. The Headman understood me. Then I marked the ridge, and beyond, the creek-crossings where there were no villages. I showed him how to go south to a large river which carried much bright dust.

"The Headman nodded, but let me see that the saldu wanted to sleep where they were. I made gestures to show that the houses were damp but that we would take them to a good place to sleep. During this hand-talk, we saw that they carried neither bows nor spears. Instead, each one wore a curved knife in his belt, of a material we do not have, and a black stick, with a second stick in the hand. One saldu pointed his stick at the watgurwa, which was empty. The stick exploded with a voice of thunder and a cloud of smoke. When the smoke blew off there was a hole in the side of the watgurwa. We did not move or change our eyes, either then or after, while the Headman spoke with the one who had done this, but it was thus we learned of the firesticks of the saldu.

"We led the Headman to a cave below the village. It was dry, and we brought firewood. Soon all the saldu were seated around a fire there, laughing and talking and drinking some herb tea they appeared to like very much. They made signs to me to take them to our women. I shook my head and pointed over the ridge. And because no baby cried and no sound came from the houses, they believed our women were not with us.

"We kept a watch all night. They quarreled and two of them fought with knives. The Headman stopped them, threatening them with his firestick. Soon they slept. They left the next morning. We were glad to see them go, and Elder Uncle and Younger Son, your father, followed them to be sure they did not return.

"They went out of sight over the ridge, but after awhile we heard the distant boumf! of one of their firesticks. We could only wonder what this might mean, but Elder Uncle and your father, who were following them, found the body of one of the People from a village on Banya Creek. We learned afterward he had been out alone, praying, and so missed our lookout who went during the night to warn the Banya Creek villages.

"The snow was red with blood where he lay. He had been scalped. Elder Uncle emptied his quiver to use as a cover for his head."

Grandfather said a prayer and blew some tobacco smoke from his stone pipe toward Waganupa, as a sign the story was finished.

"Then what did my father and my uncle do?" Ishi asked.

"Su, su! I am weary of thinking about the saldu. Do you answer the wanasi's question, my Elder Son."

Elder Uncle said, "Can one trust this wanasi not to tell his cousin?"

"Elder Brother of my father, have I ever told the secrets of the watgurwa?"

"Su! Do not be angry. You are young; you have slept in the watgurwa for only a brief while. But you tell no secrets and one day you will be such a hunter as was your father. . . . . As for the saldu—Younger Brother and I followed them which was no great matter. Their four-footers could barely move on our trails which are meant for the feet of men. There were fresh drops of blood in the snow along the trail and soon we saw that this blood came from the scalp of our friend, which one saldu, riding at a distance behind the others, wore on his belt.

"Younger Brother circled around him and shot him with a single arrow. The saldu fell from his horse into the soft snow with no cry or other sound. I waved my arms and the horse shied and left the trail, going off into the brush.

37

"After some time, we heard three boumf, boumf, boumfs of a firestick. As we now know, this was a signal to the missing one. But no saldu returned to look for him. . . . They would not have found him in any case; we hid him well enough. Those others left the Yahi World; we saw no more of them.

"We carried the body of our friend to his own village. He and his scalp were together; his Spirit would not wander the hills looking for what had been taken from him. . . . Now you know how those first ones came 'out of the mountain,' as Grandmother says."

The next day, Ishi hunted and caught a rabbit for Mother. She made a stew of deer jerky and the rabbit. He ate some of the stew and dipped the hard acorn bread of winter into his broth. Grandfather looked at him from time to time, wondering what were the young hunter's thoughts. Grandfather decided Ishi looked as usual.

But his thoughts were not as usual. He touched his bow. *I must pray to Jupka and Kaltsuna, Maker of Arrows. My arrows shoot straight. They will hit any saldu who comes within range of my bow.*

All that night and for many nights, saldu stalked Ishi's dreams, threatening to scalp him. But his arrows went straight. The saldu of his dreams lay still.

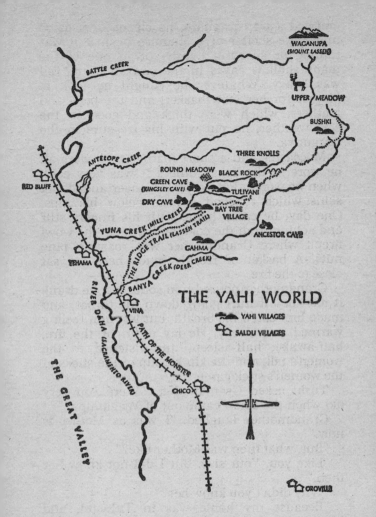

THE YAHI WORLD

- YAHI VILLAGES
- SALDU VILLAGES

AS LONG as there was daylight, Ishi usually spent the winter days somewhere between Black Rock and Tuliyani, setting snares under rocks, in the snow, in bushes; and laying traps on the runways of the small four-footers and birds who, like him, were awake and hunting. Having

39

emptied a trap or snare, he cleaned his catch under the shelter of a chamise bush if it was raining or snowing lightly, or in one of the many shallow caves in the canyon if the fall was heavy. Whatever he caught he took to Mother for her stew basket; and the pelts and feathers, which were thick and good in the cold weather, he put with his treasure in the watgurwa.

Moccasins and a short feather cape were all he wore in the brush unless it was very cold, when he wore a long cape of badger and skunk skins which reached a little below his hips. One day, he came home with his fingers stiff and aching from the cold, and went to the wowi firepit where Grandmother was roasting pine nuts. A basket of freshly made herb tea sat close to the fire.

Grandmother poured him some tea; he drank it too hot—it hurt going down his throat, and made him catch his breath, but left him feeling warmed and sleepy. He lay down by the fire, half-awake, half-asleep, and listened to the women's talk and the klp klp klp of the sticks of the women's stick game.

Tushi asked Grandmother, "Were you very old when the saldu came out of Waganupa?"

Grandmother laughed. "I was as Mother is now."

"But, what then was Mother like?"

"Like you. Your size. But I did not know her then."

"Why didn't you know her?"

"Because my home was in Tuliyani, and Mother's in Gahma, a long way off on Banya Creek. I knew Mother first when my Younger Son brought her home as his wife."

They were playing the stick game. Grandmother put her hands behind her back and Tushi guessed which hand held the single white counter among the bundle of red ones. Tushi chose the hand which held only red, so Grandmother kept the sticks and scratched a "win" with a piece of bone on a smooth rock beside her.

Said Grandmother, teasing Tushi, "Tck, tck, a woman must play the stick game well. She needs to learn what the eyes of the other player say, and she must know how to count so she will know how much she has lost or won—and how many shells are in her necklace."

"I know how many shells are in my necklace!"

Ishi was counting. *When Mother was as big as Tushi, the hills and the river-valley were filled with people. There were other worlds too, to the south and east and north and west. . . . Last night Elder Uncle said only Yahi were left in the hills when I was born. And three turnings of the moons ago, when Elder Uncle brought us to Tuliyani, there were not even any Yahi left but us.*

The next morning, Timawi and Ishi were bringing in wood for the watgurwa fire and Ishi asked, "Why could not the People turn away the other saldu as Grandfather turned away the first ones?"

Timawi answered, "There were too many of them; they came too fast. So Elder Uncle says, Grandfather says it was because all saldu carried firesticks and hunted the People, meaning to empty the hills of us."

"Why then were not all the Yahi killed as were the others?"

"I think it was because your father learned to fight the enemy. And once he learned this, they stopped coming over the ridge trail and through Yahi country since they might be shot down by the arrows of the wanasi. Your father taught the People—not only the wanasi, but the old, the children and the women—to hide at the back of dark caves, under piles of leaves, in the middle of a clump of poison oak or spiny manzanita. He showed them how to lie face-down beside a trail, sometimes with a rock to hide them, sometimes with nothing. Horses might pass almost over them without their being discovered.

"He and the good swimmers learned to stay for a long time under water against a boulder, or to swim into the shade where they could come up to breathe as a bullfrog does, and go under without being seen. The wanasi with your father even learned to go behind water-falls while saldu searched and then gave up the search because they could not see them behind the water."

"Tell me what else my father did."

"I heard him say in the watgurwa, 'Jupka and Kaltsuna gave us no weapons for fighting men, but the saldu do not have a magic which turns the straight-flying arrow from their hearts; it may enter as it enters the deer's heart.' "

"Did my father's and the other wanasi's arrows enter the hearts of many saldu?"

"Not many, not enough; the Yahi were the hunted ones. But many times, your father drew the enemy away from the villages, from the women and children and Old Ones who were without bow and arrows. He did this by show-ing himself, he and his wanasi, by leaving signs where they had made a fire. But they kept out of range of the saldu firesticks. I remember one time when they were gone for more than two moons. Your father led a large party of saldu around the foot of Waganupa to the far side. In all that time, the saldu did not kill a single Yahi, did not take a single scalp. Finally, your father turned south and left the saldu well outside the Yahi World and so came safely home with all his men. Aii-ya! If I had been of a size to go with him! To have shot my arrows into the enemy!"

"And then what did my father do?"

"You have heard Elder Uncle say, 'One man cannot forever hold against twenty saldu with firesticks.' That is what he tried to do at Three Knolls Village where he fell."

The next day, Ishi caught a fat marmot. Only a foot was in the light trap which it had dragged into the brush, and Ishi shot it with his bow. *I know now why Elder Uncle says a bow is better than a trap. The arrow kills; a trap may cause only fear and pain.*

He cleaned the marmot and put it in his basket. Instead of going home, he went to Black Rock. He wished to think about his father; about the Yahi World. When he had relived all Timawi had told him and made pictures before his eyes of that moons-long trip around Waganupa which his father had led, his thoughts came back again to Black Rock.

Three Knolls Village is behind me; Tuliyani, below; Gahma, far away in Banya Canyon. These are the villages I know.

I remember a Harvest Feast, when I sat on Mother's lap and hid my face from all the people who were there. So many faces, strange faces, twenty, thirty of them. I never thought there were so many people in the whole world.

Ishi blew tobacco from the open palm of his hand toward Waganupa, and to the Earth Directions, west, north, east and south, saying a prayer. Then he sat back on Black Rock with his eyes closed, thinking of his brave father. Much later he opened his eyes, surprised that he was still on Black Rock, and with his cape wrapped close around him against a cold wind. The Monster called, far-away and lonesome, and Sun went under the edge of the earth, his headdress red as a redheaded woodpecker. Ishi picked up his basket with the marmot.

Mother will like this fat one.

He ran home in the winter dark, and Elder Uncle met him as he came near the village. He put a hand on Ishi's shoulder. "Where were you all this time, Younger Brother's Son? I have been uneasy for you."

"I went to a secret praying place, Elder Uncle. There, a dream came to me which I do not understand. I prayed for wisdom to fight the saldu, but the dream brought no wisdom."

"Put it out of your thoughts until later—then tell it to me."

After the evening meal, Elder Uncle made an excuse to get something from the storehouse and took Ishi with him. "Tell me your dream now, Tehna-Ishi."

"This is not the first time I have dreamed. The dream is always of going to the Great Valley where the Monster comes beside the River Daha. In the dream today, I was sitting near the rim of the canyon as when I was awake. Then I was no longer there. I was in Yuna Creek, willing my way under the snow and into the water. Down, down I went, swimming, over the falls, through the gorge of the canyon, out of the hills and the Yahi World and across the Great Valley.

"This time I did not stop there, but I was carried into the River Daha and down that river to the Gathering of Waters Grandfather speaks of, and on into Outer Ocean.

"In Outer Ocean, the Sacred Salmon was waiting for me. I stayed with him until the snow moons were gone and it was the time of the New Year and the green clover moon. I came home with Salmon then, swimming as he swam from Outer Ocean into the River Daha, into Yuna Creek which was running high as it does in spring, up over the falls and on and on, leaping among the boulders as does Salmon.

"Then I woke up. I was above the canyon once more; it was cold; and Sun was going under the edge of the earth."

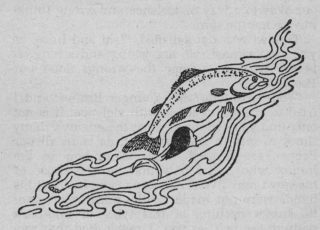

Elder Uncle kept a hand on Ishi's shoulder. His voice was gentle. "Bend the bow within your stretch, my Son. Use in your sling, rocks which fit your hand. And do not guess what the Gods intend by the dreams they send. I do not know what your dream means, but it is a Power Dream. Follow the Way, and in the moons to come you will learn its meaning. . . . It is cold, let us go inside."

When Timawi had made a fire in the watgurwa and the three men and Ishi were sitting by it, Elder Uncle said, "We talk here too much of the saldu. It is for you, Grandfather, to teach Timawi and Ishi all that has to do with the Gods and Heroes, for you are full of wisdom. I must give them the wanasi skills of hand and foot and eye and nose. For the rest, they should learn to shun the enemy in their thoughts as they avoid him in the meadows and the brush."

45

Timawi spoke when Elder Uncle was finished. "Would you have us forget what the saldu did to the People? Do you forget?"

"Forget? Timawi, you speak like a marimi, a woman. . . . . To remember, and to turn from our Way to a way of violence and wrong thinking are not the same."

Timawi was not satisfied. "Ishi and I are, as you say, wanasi; we are young and strong. It is our wish to avenge the wrongs done our People."

"You two alone? My Younger Brother and I tried to answer violence with violence. It is not only that you are two against the enemy's many times twenty in number. You, as were all our People, are trained to the silent bow of the hunter who hunts only that he and those of his wowi may live. The weapons he holds in his hands were not made for the hunting of men; he knows nothing of this tying of another's scalp to the belt, as you, Timawi, tied that raccoon tail to your belt.

"I do not forget the destroyers of the People; I do not forget the saldu who left my Younger Brother unmoving before his own house, who would hunt us out if they knew we yet live. But not all—not most—saldu are dawana, dangerous. There are saldu who wish us no harm, who take no scalps, who hunt only to eat; whose Way is one of peace. Remember this, Timawi and Ishi, in the moons to come when I shall not be here to remind you."

Ishi asked, "Why, then, my Uncle, do not these saldu stop their dawana ones from doing evil?"

"I do not know, Tehna-Ishi. I think I am too old to understand the saldu, and you are too young. But you will not always be young. . . . . Perhaps the saldu were not well taught by their

46

Old Ones. Perhaps they forgot their teachings on the long journey across the deserts."

Wrapped in his rabbitskin blanket, close to Elder Uncle, Ishi listened to the sleeping-breathing of the men. He ached in his arms, in his legs, in his head. Elder Uncle's words said themselves over and over.

To be wanasi, almost grown-up, is not an easy thing. With his hand on his bow, he slept, and his dream was of Tushi. Her cheeks were red like the toyon berry and she wore her shell necklace with the new flower beads. She ran through deep snowdrifts and as she ran, dawana saldu raised their firesticks against her. They wanted Tushi's scalp. Running, running, he shot arrow after arrow, but they fell short and disappeared in the deep snowdrifts. He had no more arrows and he dug and dug in the snow but he could not find his arrows.

Ishi shook himself awake. *Elder Uncle is right. It is not good thinking always of the enemy.*

He lay on his back, staring wide-awake at the circle of the Sky World he could see through the smokehole. There, at the top of the sky, were the Five Star Sisters, dancing. *I knew the Star Sisters before I knew the Monster. My father showed them to me. I looked and laughed because he pointed to them and laughed. Always since that time, I want to laugh when I see them.*

He turned on his side and slept. No more dawana saldu came in his dreams; only the Star Sisters were there, dancing, dancing.

"THE SNOW moons stay on past their proper turn," said Grandfather, shivering with cold. "It is as when the saldu first came."

It was time for the spring run of salmon, for green clover, for deer to be returning from the mountain with their newborn fawns; time for the old earth to shake off its snow blanket and begin a New Year for its People.

But there was ice in the canyon where Sun did not reach; there were no deer, no green buds, no clover. Mother scraped the bottom of the food baskets which had been full at harvest time. Timawi and Ishi put out more trap lines; they dug with sticks into burrows; they brought home what they could—a snow bird, a field mouse, a chipmunk—for Mother to put into her stew, made now of the last of the acorns, which tasted old and stale.

One morning, Ishi lay flat on a rock outcrop, scraping off the lichen which grew over the rock. It would help to flavor Mother's stew, and perhaps Timawi would find something; he had gone to an old badger hole to see if there might be a four-footer asleep there.

As Ishi scraped, he practiced brush talk. He squeaked like a field mouse, smacked like a rabbit, chattered like a squirrel. A small cotton-tail rabbit came out of the brush, hopping closer and closer to him. Ishi put down his scraper and cupped his hands on the rock, smacking his lips softly. With a last hop, rabbit landed between Ishi's hands. There it wriggled itself down, its ears folded back. Ishi lifted the rabbit to his face. The beat of the heart brushed the soft fur back and forth against his cheek, not the uneven pounding of fear, but a steady beat, beat, beat.

Timawi called, "Yagka yagka!" He wanted Ishi to come. Ishi set the little rabbit on the ground. *I am hungry. My People are hungry. It is the duty of the hunter to take what he can. But this four-footer I shall not take. It came to me without fear, knowing I was not hunting.*

Ishi found Timawi in a bare oak tree where he and a wide-awake gray squirrel were answering each other in identical scolding voices. Squirrel would not come near him, nor would it stay still long enough for Timawi to use his sling or his bow. He pointed to an alder tree downhill from the oak, and when Ishi was ready with an arrow notched on his bowstring, Timawi shook the oak as hard as he could. Squirrel took a long leap toward the alder; Ishi shot it as it landed. They skinned the squirrel and took it home, Ishi wearing the bushy tail in his belt.

Mother put the squirrel and the lichen in

her soup basket, but she shook her head. Grandfather and Grandmother sat close to the fire. They were never really warm these days when there was not enough to eat. Ishi saw how their hands shook when they held out their baskets to be filled.

Later, when he brought wood to Mother's fire, he said, "The Old should not be hungry."

"The Young should not be hungry," was Mother's answer. "It is deer liver and fat salmon and the oil of fresh nuts which makes bones grow strong and straight."

Mother eats less than any of us. She moves her hand from her basket to her mouth to finish with us. But there is nothing in it. . . . Elder Uncle is more careful to thank Mother for the food in the days of hunger than in the days of much food. Yesterday he said, "Only you, My Younger Brother's Wife, can make such mush from the bitter acorn." Today, he said, "You have good wanasi to hunt for you; at your firepit we eat fresh squirrel stew in the time of the late snow moon."

The next morning was still, clear, bitter cold. Ishi and Timawi visited their traps; there was nothing in any of them. They tied their belts tighter, trying not to think of their hunger. They came home with one nest of mice. The birds and four-footers, like Grandfather and Grandmother by the fire, stayed in their nests and holes, waiting hungrily for the New Year.

Mother made a stew of the few little mice and a handful of acorn flour: it was all they had to eat that day. Elder Uncle did not suggest going to the watgurwa; the men would stay at Mother's fire until they could hunt again.

The women sat playing the stick game; no one spoke of being hungry. Ishi and Timawi were chewing sinew for bowstrings. Ishi asked, "Elder Uncle, why is it we have a hunting bow, but no fighting bow, no bow meant for the enemy?"

"It is because of a battle—the first battle in the world—which took place between two Heroes of the Olden Times. It is a tale to interest men; but women have their game, so I will tell it to you. . . . The Heroes were called Ahalamila and Jikula. All was well between them until they both wished to marry the daughter of Moon. She chose Ahalamila. Theirs was a house of peace, and a son was born to them, named Topuna.

"But Jikula did not forget; he waited his chance for revenge, and this chance came in the spring. Ahalamila led the hunters who were to kill deer and bring them to the God Jupka. Jikula used a powerful magic which made the deer invisible. For a whole moon Ahalamila and the others searched in brush and meadows, and at last turned home without having seen a single deer. There was grumbling among the hunters.

"Jikula then boasted of his magic, even as they were going home, and a battle began between Ahalamila and his men and Jikula and his men—the first battle in the world. They fought with their spears and slings and bows. Many on both sides were killed, and Jikula killed Ahalamila. The battle might have gone on until all those who fought were dead, but Jupka heard the noise and came to where they were fighting. Throwing himself between the lines of fighters, he shouted, 'It is enough! Return, all of you, to your watgurwa.' And so the battle ended."

Elder Uncle paused; Timawi had a question. "The Heroes must have learned much in that battle about fighting. What was said in the watgurwa councils?"

"They learned something, Timawi. In the watgurwa, Jupka and Kaltsuna agreed to give the Yahi People only hunting weapons, and to teach them to live in peace with each other and with their neighbors."

Two long lines of Yahi Heroes fighting with slings and spears and bows! . . . . With a hunting bow, my father fought against twenty saldu.

Grandmother put down her red sticks and said, "That is not the end of the story."

"It becomes a woman's tale," replied Grandfather.

"Then a woman may tell it. . . . Topuna lived with his Grandmother. He said to her, 'Mother of my father, why do you cry?'

" 'I cry because there is no one to avenge your father's death.'

" 'Give me my father's bows, Grandmother,'

"She brought them to him. He chose the strongest of them, the one with string made from the shoulder sinew of a male deer; and he practiced until he could shoot this bow as had his father. One day, Jikula went to hunt birds, concealing himself in a tree. Topuna, unseen by Jikula, hid in the tree next to his. There, he made the call of the redheaded woodpecker, the whirr of the humming bird, and the song of the yellow finch. Jikula moved closer and closer; and his foot stuck out from the leaves of the tree. Topuna shot, his arrow entering Jikula's heel with such force that he fell to the ground where he lay, unable to move.

"Then Topuna shot another arrow and another, pinning Jikula down with a double row of arrows, up one side and down the other. He called to his Grandmother who came running. When she saw what her Grandson had done, she danced round and round Jikula, singing, 'Jikula will rise no more. Jikula who killed my son the Hero Ahalamila, will kill no more.' So died the Hero Jikula."

When my new hunting bow is finished, and Elder Uncle says I may bend it, I shall be as Topuna with his Father's bow. . . . Timawi and I are not like the Heroes Ahalamila and Jikula—we live in peace as Jupka said we should. Let the enemy then stay out of our canyons; away from our watgurwa and our wowi, from our Old Ones, our Majapa, our Mother and our Cousin. If they come, Timawi and I remember my father; we remember Topuna.

TUSHI was asleep by the time Grandmother finished the story of Topuna, but hunger kept the others on the edge of sleep. The fire burned down; there was no sound, no movement.

Then—it was past the middle of the night—there was a rush and roar and the earth-covered house shook. The pine and fir trees of the high slopes screamed and cracked as winds tore through them and came moaning down the canyon and whirled into Tuliyani.

Smoke and dust blew down the smokehole, filling the wowi, choking those inside. Timawi piled dry wood on the fire, which blazed up and forced the smoke and dust out. The Yahi, old and young, smiled as they listened to the crash of falling limbs and the whine of the wind through the trees. Spring had come, brought by the Big

53

Winds of Waganupa, as it had come since the beginning of the world.

In the morning, the houses and paths were covered with broken branches and pine needles, and the drying frames were knocked over, and Ishi's snares and traps were smashed and tangled. With the rising of Sun the winds left Tuliyani; a warm, quiet rain followed the winds. There was nothing to eat that day. Grandmother brewed a strong herb tea and they drank it instead of food.

All day and all night the warm rain fell, while under the warming earth the New Year was born: pale shoots from sleeping bulbs and seeds pushed their way to the light.

In the morning, Sun's colored plumes waved high into the Sky World, pouring warmth over the wakening earth. And on the dun-brown hills, up and down the canyon walls, over bare boulders and rocks, sprouted new, tender clover. It was the New Year, the time of the green clover moon.

The snow on Waganupa melted and filled the streams with rushing white water for five days. The clover grew to a size for gathering and eating, and after five risings and settings of Sun, the waters of the creek became quieter. Timawi and Ishi raced each other from the watgurwa to the creek, into the creek and down, out of sight. Up again, out of the water, shouting and waving, they held high in their hands two salmon, twisting with life, gleaming with the colors of the moon—the Sacred Salmon, which return each springtime from Outer Ocean up the River Daha into Yuna Creek.

More and more salmon swam upstream against the current. Timawi and Ishi harpooned them when they tired of catching the fish with their hands. They filled baskets and brought them to Mother, racing back to the creek for more.

The evening meal was cooked in the open after Sun was gone. It was a feast, and Mother, too, ate the sea-fresh fish and tender green clover. Old and young ate of the foods of spring and the New Year. They gave thanks to Salmon; and they saved the bones, placing them close to the fire to dry. Later, when these bones were ground to flour, they would eat them, so that some of the power and strength of the salmon would enter their bodies.

For twice five days Ishi was in the creek in water to his waist or higher, fishing, fishing. He went underwater. He swam upstream, strong against the current, as Salmon swims. Breathless, he pulled himself out of the water onto a boulder in mid-stream, where he lay gasping like a stranded fish. The spray washed over him and the gleaming arrow-bodies of the salmon rushed past him, leaping out of the water. He was back in his dream, swimming, leaping homeward from Outer Ocean.

I am hungry. I am the fisherman for my People. I am Salmon! I leap, always upstream, against the current, from Outer Ocean to my home on Yuna Creek!

While Ishi lived the early springtime, half-fish half-Yahi, Mother and Grandmother and Tushi lived the Yahi woman's springtime.

Mother scrubbed the storage baskets, then put them on their sides toward Sun to dry. Grandmother spread the fur and feather capes and rugs and blankets of rabbit and bearskin where Sun shone on them. She rubbed sand into the fur, then brushed it out again to clean them. When they were well sunned, she rolled them in grass mats and laid them on shelves in a shady storehouse. The spring and heat and harvest moons would grow old before the feathers and furs would be unrolled.

After each meal, Tushi spread the salmon bones on a mat in the sun until they were dry. Then she put them in a stone mortar and ground them to flour. Ishi and Timawi, on the way to the creek with their harpoons, stopped to watch her. Sweat glistened on her arms and legs and body; her bark skirt went shu shu, and the shells of her necklace swayed and rattled as she worked. She straightened up to push her basket-hat back and brush the hair out of her eyes. The shell beads lay quiet and white against her throat.

She is the pretty one, the gentle one—White Shell Girl. She is like the young girl in Grand-

mother's story: her father made a feast for her in the time of the green clover moon, and because she was young and dambusa the People danced for her all around the rim of the world.

I wish there were many People; then we could dance round the rim of the world for Tushi.

When the grinding was done, Mother and Grandmother and Tushi took digging sticks and went up and down hill, picking, gathering, digging, coming home with full baskets. They gathered clover and other greens to cook with fresh deermeat stew. They dug young bulbs, some sweet, some peppery. They picked irises and ferns. On the sunny hillsides were poppies and lupines; in the deep shade, violets and trilliums.

Above the blossoms fluttered the jupka butterfly and other butterflies whose black and orange and brown wings reminded Tushi of the patterns she was learning to weave into baskets. As far as they could see, the hills were covered with a soft mat of clover and bright flowers, with butterflies hovering over them. Their baskets full, the women of Tuliyani sat for awhile in the sun, enjoying the flowers and the butterflies; and they saw that the Yahi World was dambusa, as Jupka had meant them to see it.

The first spring salmon run was over; the clover was beginning to grow coarse and tough. Elder Uncle said to Ishi, "Tomorrow you shall bend your bow. It is time to hunt the spring deer; better now before the saldu are upon them with their firesticks, and the deer run away, frightened, to the mountain."

The bow was finished; it had been seasoning for two moons. Ishi had fasted before each step in its making. He had gone to a prayer place in the junipers above Three Knolls to pray and cut wood for the sacred fire in the watgurwa. Under Grandfather's instruction he had shaped, bent, polished his bow and backed it with sinew. Grandfather said it was more strongly backed than many bows of greater length and weight.

"To have a strong singing bow," said Grand-

57

father, "keep the bow lying on deerskin or in its own cover whenever it is not being carried. It belongs in the watgurwa, not in the wowi. And it should lie on its back, not on its face. Never leave your bow standing—it will sweat and become tired and weak; it will no longer be a strong-shooting bow. It needs rest as does the hunter."

Ishi ate nothing the morning of the first bending of his bow. He went to his prayer place before it was light, running all the way there and back. He prayed to Kaltsuna, Maker of Arrows. He took a sweatbath in the watgurwa and swam in the creek. Elder Uncle and Grandfather and Timawi watched while he strung his bow for the first time and then slowly bent it to its full draw.

"Aiku tsub! It is good!" Ishi's bow took the form of the crescent moon.

"Now!" Elder Uncle pointed to a rotten stump. Ishi shot an arrow low along the ground which pierced the stump, dead center. His next shot was made squatting, only the soles of his feet touching the ground. He shot far to the left, far to the right in this position. Then, standing, he shot high overhead, his arrow hitting the farthest waving maple leaf which Elder Uncle named as the target.

"Aiku tsub. Aiku tsub. The arrows go straight and true." Elder Uncle gave Ishi a cover for his bow, made from a mountain lion's tail. "Take this which I made for you; cover and guard well your bow. You are a true wanasi. When the men of Tuliyani go to hunt the deer you will go with them. And if the enemy comes, you will shoot your bow as your father shot his."

The first time Ishi took his new bow to Black Rock, he held it to his lips, touching the string lightly. He sang an ancient Yahi song to the singing string.

Hini—yasha!
Ru—hi—yamba!
Bi—hanya!
Hini—yasha!
Hini—yasha!

Going—sings!
Following—deer trail!
Hunting—deer!
Going—sings!
Going—sings!

He waited until the Monster came and went in the distant valley. *My new bow must know the Monster as my old bow knows him!*

ELDER UNCLE *says I may shoot the first deer of the New Year! Timawi and I go to hunt today! We—the wanasi of Tuliyani. We have fasted and prayed and taken the before-hunting bath. Long moons away, when I have brought to the village many deer, they will call me Ishi the Hunter.*

Hini—yasha!
Ru—hi—yamba!

All night Ishi talked in his sleep to his bow; he and Timawi were on their way before dawn. They rinsed their mouths with clean water, but took no food. They would eat only after their return from the hunt.

Each wanasi carried in his broad deerskin belt his sharpest rockglass knife, sheathed in moleskin. A full quiver hung over the right shoulder and down the back, while three arrows besides were under the left arm, in reach without changing position. They took with them also a length of rope, a basket and a stuffed deer's head.

They began to smell deer before they reached Three Knolls. Keeping downwind, they circled the knolls, sniffing, listening, testing the air and the ground for any sign of saldu. They signaled each other only by bird and animal calls. At last, satisfied there were no saldu, Timawi hid behind one of the knolls and Ishi crouched, his bow bent and ready, in a clump of scrub oak, a little downhill from Timawi.

Timawi began with bird and rabbit talk. Two buck deer were at the edge of the heavy brush. Timawi made some fawn cries; the deer looked up, but went back to their feeding. He covered the top of his own head with the deer head, raised himself so the head was in plain sight, then bobbed it up and down and turned it from side to side as if he were looking and tasting. Now the bucks were interested; they sniffed the air; they found nothing alarming. They stopped feeding and moved closer to the strange nodding head.

The range was good, as they came in toward Timawi, and not too far. Ishi shot without changing his crouching position. He shot too high; the arrow whizzed skimmingly across the back of the lead buck like a bird flying across him and lodged in a bay tree. The buck flicked an ear at the arrow as he would at a bird; he moved on toward Timawi. Ishi shot again; this arrow went deep, a good shot below the shoulder. The deer threw his head up, took a staggering step. Then the head lowered, the legs bent; he lay on the ground.

Ishi came quickly but without stir or noise, pulling the knife from its sheath as he came.

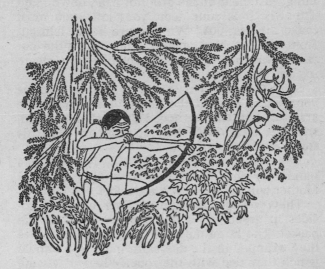

With one strong cut across the throat of the dying deer, the kill was complete. The other deer and the birds and rabbits which had been close by disappeared into the heavier brush: they smelled blood and death, as when the mountain lion makes its kill. But there was no panic, no crashing or running—nothing was amiss in the brush world. The second buck went back to nibbling the young tree shoots which his interest in the nodding head had interrupted.

For a moment, Ishi stood alone over the fallen deer. He said in a low voice, "I give you thanks, Waganupa, Mountain of the Center of the World, for sending to me this deer. I give you thanks, Kaltsuna, Maker of Arrows, for guiding my arrow." These were the first words he had spoken since they left the canyon.

Timawi came up and together they tied the rope around the deer, then threw an end over a strong oak limb and hoisted the body up until it hung, just clear of the ground, head down. Said Timawi, "It is your deer, your kill—you must make the first cut." With a sure hand, Ishi cut from tail to chin, opening the belly—the cut which was the beginning of the bleeding, cleaning and skinning.

Said Timawi, "This one fell at once because your arrow pierced the heart." He handed the arrow to Ishi who removed the rockglass head, wiped it clean with leaves, and put it in his treasure pouch.

When the deer was skinned, Ishi ran his hand over the hide. "It is without a blemish. Mother will have a new warm skirt this winter."

They wrapped the heart, liver and soft insides in green grass and packed them in the basket. The large pieces of meat and the bones they wrapped in the deerskin, making a bundle which they tied with the rope. When they were finished, they spread fresh earth and rocks and leaves on the ground under the oak tree; no signs of the day's butchering and cleaning remained.

Once during the day a saldu passed on the rim trail close to them. They lay face-down without moving, as the clup clup of burro hooves could be heard more and more plainly. Perhaps the burro smelled them; he shied, and there followed the noise of scraping against a thorn bush, of a pan falling with a clatter and of a raised saldu voice; and then the strangled unhappy-sounding bray of the burro.

As soon as the clup clup of the hooves was resumed, going on up the trail, the two hunters climbed the bay tree into which Ishi's first arrow had gone. They saw a bearded saldu leading a burro loaded with blanket roll, pick and shovel, black cookpot and the pan and wooden cradle used to wash the bright dust from the creeks. The saldu smelled nothing unusual; his eyes remained on the trail.

"He thinks of nothing but the bright dust which will bring him power," Ishi remarked of him.

Said Timawi, "All saldu four-footers have strange voices—the burro, the horse and the cow. Only the loon bird among us, has such a harsh cry."

"So are saldu voices harsh and strange." They practiced the burro bray, but softly. Elder Uncle did not allow them to use it in the canyon; it might bring saldu there.

Ishi remembered to pull his arrow from the tree. *A hunter retrieves his arrow. It takes much work to make an arrow, and the arrowhead is treasure.*

It was dark when Timawi and Ishi came into Tuliyani with the first load of spring deer.

During the second moon of the New Year, the men went out from the watgurwa to hunt deer, while Mother and Grandmother and Tushi dug the fresh white roots of camas and anise and of brodiaea and many other bulb plants. Sometimes, they wrapped the new-dug roots in maple leaves and packed them in the hot ashes in the firepit, with more leaves over the top and then a layer of hot rocks. There the roots baked slowly all day, and at the evening meal Mother gave each person a bundle of several kinds of baked roots in their wrapping of maple leaves.

Cherries and plums ripened in the late spring. There were mushrooms to be gathered from places of deep shade while they were pale and tender. And one by one, the different berries ripened as the days grew warmer, and each in its season was picked to be eaten fresh or dried.

It would not rain again until after the heat and harvest moons grew old and gave place to the fog and rain and snow moons of late autumn and winter. Sun shone hotter and longer each day. Poppies and lupins faded; seedpods formed where blossoms had been. The spring mat of green on the hills turned yellow, then sunburned to golden-brown. The grass and the sun-darkened bodies of the People of Tuliyani were the same color.

Old and young, they liked the heat moons. They slept under the open sky and worked in the light shade of leaf canopies which stirred with any breeze. They wore no clothes, and even Grandfather and Grandmother swam in Yuna Creek each day. Timawi and Ishi swam before and after hunting, while they were fishing, and after Sun was gone and the hot land began to cool. They swam across the creek and back, and for longer distances up and downstream, keeping their eyes open underwater, learning where the sharp boulders were and where the deep pools in which trout hid.

Tushi swam with them. If the water was swift or deep, she clung to Ishi's long hair.

Timawi and Ishi climbed up and down the walls of the gorge of the canyon on ropes, dropping into the water noiselessly as water snakes. Even when the canyon was like a firepit and the nights still and hot, no one cared. This fierce heat was part of life; it was a time to rest between the long days and nights of hunting and fishing and gathering during the spring and harvest times. It made the hungry days and nights of winter distant and unreal.

"Why is nothing said in the watgurwa of going to Waganupa?" Ishi asked Timawi. "We have always gone during the heat moons; all Yahi before us have always gone."

"Elder Uncle has decided it is not safe to go. Everywhere there are saldu, nor can Grandfather and Grandmother run or climb trees to escape them, nor lie for days in a dark cave, hiding. And these things we would almost surely have to do on the mountain."

"Then what of the fall deer which we must have if we are not to starve during the snow moons—the deer will not stay in the lower hills with the cracking of firesticks in the air."

"Perhaps Elder Uncle and we two may go."

"We two could go alone?"

"Elder Uncle fears we might—if the chance came—do like Topuna and avenge ourselves on the enemy."

"Would you, Timawi?"

"Yes. I cannot agree in my heart with Elder Uncle."

Many times Timawi and I speak in this way. I wish to go with him; to avenge my father and my People. But—Elder Uncle is the Majapa— there cannot be division in the watgurwa. Also —what is a vengeance against one, or five, or twice five saldu? It does not bring back the People.

The heat moons passed; Sun no longer stood

so high in the sky as in the beginning of summer; shadows were long and cool in the canyon. Manzanita berries and acorns and hazel nuts and pine nuts were ripe. The brown-red of ripe buckeye nuts shone through their husks. Elder Uncle and the two wanasi went to hunt on the mountain, as late as they dared. The hunting was good; they hid in caves during the day, hunting only at night and making caches of deer meat which Timawi and Ishi brought in to Tuliyani, also at night. It was nothing like the old way of hunting on the mountain, which was a happy time for hunters and women and children, but it meant there would be meat in the baskets.

Ducks and geese and whistling swans stopped off for a few days in Round Meadow. *Tushi and I lie on the meadow grass, watching these high-flying birds follow their leader into the Sky World. They go from north to south during the harvest moons and south to north in the green clover moons, as the People used to follow their Majapa to the mountain, then back to the canyon. They follow their leader as the duck and goose feathers of an arrow follow the rockglass arrowhead.*

The harvest moons shone once again, full and bright. It was time to pick the last of the acorns, to fill the baskets; time to make everything tight against the rain and snow moons; time to celebrate the Harvest Feast.

2

THE CAVE

THREE times the moons of all the seasons grew full and old. Three times the New Year wakened the Yahi World from its winter sleep.

Elder Uncle sometimes called Ishi "Younger Brother" now that his nose plug was the width of two fingers above that of his uncle when they stood side by side. "Younger Brother was two fingers nearer the Sky World than I," said Elder Uncle.

"He is straight and slim as a young alder tree," said Grandfather to Grandmother.

"He walks like his father," said Grandmother. "His feet seem not to touch the earth."

"Also he shoots his bow as did our Younger Son, with the same wrist motion when the arrow flies from the bowstring," said Grandfather. "Not that an old woman would see it."

"Su, su! An old woman sees what she sees. This wanasi is very handsome. I remember when you were handsome and wore your hair wound on top of your head as he wears his when he has been off somewhere praying and fasting. . . . Where can he go for such long times with saldu and their four-footers everywhere as they now are?"

Grandfather did not know the answer to Grandmother's question, but this was not something to discuss with women, so he answered, "One place and another."

The spring salmon run was over; Timawi and Ishi had brought in deer; the baskets were full. It was a good time for the young wanasi to go for some risings and settings of Sun to the hills alone. Timawi had been away and was home once more. In the watgurwa, Ishi asked permission to go. Elder Uncle said, "Go, find yourself a prayer-place to dream, away from the saldu. May your dreaming be good, and bring you much Power."

Ishi left Tuliyani before dawn the next morning, while the others slept. *I shall not go to a prayer-place. Instead I shall journey to the old villages and caves Grandfather talks of. From him I know their names and something of what happened to the People at each place.*

It can be dangerous to go where the saldu attacked, where scalps were taken. *Uneasy ghosts may be there, searching for their lost treasure bundles, for their dishonored scalps, for their stolen hair.*

I could lack courage for this journey, except I asked Elder Uncle, "Did the saldu take my father's scalp?" And he answered, "No saldu's hand or knife touched my Younger Brother. A single fireball entered his back and heart." Then I asked, "His bones, where are they?" And Elder Uncle answered, "They are safe from saldu and digging animals, in Ancestor Cave in Banya Canyon." . . . *Su! I will go where the People lived and where they died. This may be the beginning of a Dream Journey.*

Alone, with his hunting bow, Ishi went on his journey. He kept to the brush except when he was deep in the canyons. He stayed off the trails, and when he had to cross one, leaped it or brushed out his footprints. He dropped nothing on the ground; he made no fire, eating hard bread and jerky which he carried with him, and the fresh bulbs and greens and early fruit which he dug or picked on the way.

He saw saldu miners with their burros, their pans and shovels. He saw saldu cows, horses, sheep, which were grazed on Yahi land. Neither they nor their dogs nor their herders saw or smelled him.

Grandfather says, "Keep downwind of the deer you hunt and of the saldu who hunts you."

He went first to Black Rock where he prayed

to Jupka and to Kaltsuna. Sun came up over Waganupa; far, far away, the Monster called, Whu—HOOH—huu.

"Are you a God, too?" Ishi asked aloud. When he blew pinches of powdered sacred tobacco to the several directions at the end of his prayers, he blew some toward the Great Valley, saying, "For you, O Monster God."

He went then to the three knolls which overlooked the village of the same name. Like the first saldu, Ishi took the steep trail into the village, but once there, he followed a path to a crumbling earth-covered house at the edge of the village close to the trees, and went inside the house.

Here I lived with my mother and my father. This is where I learned to walk like tehna, cub-bear, and my father named me for bear. This is the smokehole where Father showed me the Dancing Star Sisters in the Sky World. By this firepit, he made me my first bow. In my treasure bundle today are three of the willow arrows my father made me, feathered with hummingbird wing-feathers.

Ishi went outside his old home.

Twenty saldu and more, hidden behind the three knolls attacked the village at dawn while everyone in the houses slept. I remember my father hiding my mother and me in the trees behind the house. People screamed; the thunder of firesticks filled the air; and there was the smell of burning. Shooting from the shelter of the house wall, my father fought the enemy. It was his bow against twenty firesticks, and some saldu were among those who lay dead on the village paths.

More saldu were hidden down the creek. One of them shot and my father fell—here—in front of his house. Mother ran to him and dragged

71

*him into the brush. No one saw her through
the smoke. She and I lay beside my father on
our faces all day. She says I did not move or
cry or speak. I think I slept some of the time.*

*At last it was dark and the saldu left. Elder
Uncle and Grandfather found my mother and
me, here, beside my father, and they took us to
Tuliyani. I remember Elder Uncle's carrying me
in his arms and I remember Mother's crying.
All the way down the canyon my mother cried
and when we were in Tuliyani, my mother and
my grandmother cried all that night and for
many days and nights. I shall not forget the
tears of my mother, nor those of my father's
mother.*

*Suwa! My father's Spirit does not forget me!
I walk as my father walked. I hold my bow as
my father held his bow. The bow turns in my
hand, ever so little; my arm takes a different
position. It is my father's voice I hear saying,
"It should be thus; do it so, good, aiku tsub!"*

From Three Knolls, Ishi crossed the ridge between Yuna Creek and Banya Creek and circled
Upper Meadow to Bushki where Timawi was
born. Bushki was close to the foot of Waganupa
on a shallow stream which flowed into the
Banya lower down; no salmon came this far.

*I see why Timawi says the canyon is like a
trap into which a bear falls. Here, there is much
openness and the mountain is close; it seems
only a step to its snow-covered top from this village. Timawi says he will come with me sometime if we leave the canyons and travel around
the rim of the world.*

*It will anger Timawi to know that a saldu
cabin is now built in the middle of the old village; I think I will not tell him this.*

Ishi went down the little stream to Banya
Creek, and then on into Banya Canyon. He

stopped at the many caves in the canyon. Some had been lived in in his own lifetime, some had been used only as camping places on the way to and from the mountain, or as caches for food during harvest time.

He came to Ancestor Cave. There he prayed and left an offering of tobacco leaves on the flat stone slab inside the cave. *This is a sacred and peaceful place—not terrible like Dry Cave and Green Cave. Here, under the stone, the bones of Yahi lie, whose Spirits were released in the Sacred Fire for the Dead. There were no living Yahi here when the saldu came. And the saldu know nothing of the Ancestors.*

He went down the canyon to Gahma. Gahma was built on a half-moon of land at creek level. Deep and still, the water came to the rounded edge of the old village. *This is the village where I was born. I was only a baby when Mother and Father went to Three Knolls Village to live, but I remember something of this place from a visit Mother and Elder Uncle and I made here. We came to see my mother's parents and to celebrate a Harvest Feast with them.*

I remember the men fishing from the bank beside the watgurwa; and I remember looking from the smokehole down into the clear, dark water. Mother says Gahma was the most beautiful of the Yahi villages in the Old Days. Yahi came from everywhere to see it. They called it dambusa Gahma.

And it was at Gahma, in the house of my mother's parents, I first saw Tushi. She and I played together in Gahma, and when we were packing our bundles to return to Tuliyani, Tushi cried because we were leaving. Then Mother's mother packed a bundle for Tushi and she came with us. . . . If she had stayed in Gahma, she would have died that day.

73

When we left Gahma, we stopped at the top of the ridge to look back and wave. I see it now as it looked that day: red-earth houses close together by the water; the men harpooning and casting near the watgurwa; the women harvesting the seeds of the tarplant on the slope behind the village; the babies in their cradle baskets on their mothers' backs or propped against bushes in the shade; the small children running up and down the slope, playing or helping with the harvesting.

Mother wished we could stay in Gahma. "It is much nicer than in the canyon in Tuliyani," she said.

We went downhill where we could no longer see Gahma. We had not gone far when we heard from the other side of the ridge the explosions of many firesticks and the thod, thod of horses. We crawled on our stomachs under the brush while Elder Uncle went back to the top where he could see Gahma.

He shook his head when he came back to us. "Nothing, it is nothing," he said, but his voice was strange.

"Go, go where you are needed," said my mother. "I will take these two safely to Tuliyani." Elder Uncle left us, nor did he return to Tuliyani for many days.

Now I know what happened here. Elder Uncle told me during the last snow moons. Saldu on horseback surprised the look-out above Gahma, then rode down the slope shooting and using their long knives. No one in Gahma escaped, not those on the hillside nor those by the creek. Said Elder Uncle, "The Banya ran red with the blood of the People that day."

The water is deep and still around the half-moon of Gahma—dambusa Gahma. Perhaps in the Land of the Dead there is such a village,

74

*where one can look down into the dark water
from the smokehole of the watgurwa.*

Ishi left Gahma and the canyon. Keeping
himself hidden, he crossed Little Hollow to
Acorn Hollow where he lay in the brush close
to a house built there by a saldu.

*I know this house. On a night, seven turn-
ings of the moons ago, Grandmother, Mother,
Tushi and I waited here in the dark. Grandfather, Elder Uncle and Timawi went inside
the house and laid their best hunting bows
before a saldu there, asking by signs that in
exchange for the bows, he give back three of
our people he had taken captive that day. They
were an old woman, her daughter and her
granddaughter, who was as big as Tushi is
now.*

*The captives were in the house, too, but they
were tied and guarded by several saldu with
firesticks. The saldu took the bows, but would
not give back the three people. The place
smelled of danger and the old woman called
to Elder Uncle to go before everyone was taken.
He dared not stay. The seven of us were in the
heavy brush and darkness before the saldu
knew we were gone. They looked for us, but
their dogs did not pick up our scent and by
morning we were safe in the gorge of Yuna
Canyon.*

*Elder Uncle returned secretly to Acorn Hol-
low, but the saldu were gone, having taken the
captives with them. He tracked them to the
edge of the Valley, but could go no farther, there
being no brush cover and many saldu there.*

*Since that day, no saldu has seen us or knows
that we live concealed in the brush and boulders of our own world.*

From Acorn Hollow, Ishi went to Bay Tree
Village on the lower Yuna. Sheep and pigs

cropped and rooted in the shade of the village trees and in the old houses. *This was the first village to fall to the saldu, Grandfather says, because it is the nearest to the Great Valley.*

Soon, as on that night seven turnings of the moons ago, Ishi was deep in the gorge of Yuna Canyon. He crossed over and left the canyon to climb up to Dry Cave on the other side. *In this cave eighteen Yahi hunters were scalped— the last of the wanasi except for Timawi. I think saldu do not come here now. There is no smell of them or their dogs.*

He moved on uphill, stopping to put a pinch of sacred tobacco at the base of an old oak tree. *Here, Grandfather says, the first Yahi was hanged. Aiiya! The saldu with their ropes, their hangings! I can see how a man hangs against the sky from the high branch!*

Ishi went to Green Cave. This time he kept his eyes open and he went inside the cave. Ferns grew there and fresh water came from a clear spring. *I remember coming here with my mother to play with other children while she visited with the Old Ones. Now, beneath the ferns lie the bones of those Young Ones and of the Old Ones who were with them: there were more of the People in this cave than in Gahma. Always I see Grandfather and Elder Uncle and Timawi burying bones, burying bones.*

When Ishi left Green Cave, the brightness of Sun made him blink and put his hand up to shade his eyes.

I forgot where I was. . . . How much time has passed since the day I came here with my mother! . . . . Now I have completed the journey which I vowed to make so that I might feel under my feet the earth, the paths, the cave floors, all the places where my father and my People lived and died. I have made offerings of

76

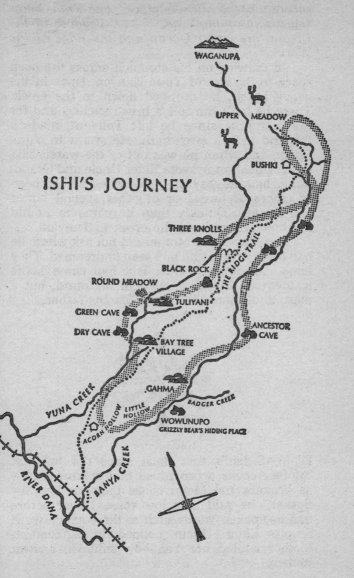

ISHI'S JOURNEY

WAGANUPA

UPPER MEADOW

BUSHKI

THREE KNOLLS

THE RIDGE TRAIL

BLACK ROCK

ROUND MEADOW

TULIYANI

GREEN CAVE

DRY CAVE

ANCESTOR CAVE

BAY TREE VILLAGE

YUNA CREEK

GAHMA

BADGER CREEK

LITTLE HOLLOW

ACORN HOLLOW

WOWUNUPO
GRIZZLY BEAR'S HIDING PLACE

BANYA CREEK

RIVER DAHA

sacred tobacco in these places, and I now know something of my land. . . . . Beyond, in the Dream, are Outer Ocean and the Edge of the World.

Ishi crawled on his stomach across the open space to the rim of Yuna Canyon. Once in the heavy brush, he dropped down to the creek. There he built himself a brush shelter, and for the first time since he left Tuliyani, made a fire and took a sweatbath. He swam in Yuna Creek, and when he was out of the water, said the purification prayers Elder Uncle and Grandfather had taught him to use when he had been in places of burial or of other special power and danger. Quickly then he came to Round Meadow and crossed the creek to Tuliyani.

Elder Uncle and Mother did not ask where he had been, or what he had seen or dreamed. They knew, whatever it was, Ishi had come home to them no longer a child in his mind, but a man; and, more than ever, like his father.

IT WAS Ishi's first meal since the journey. "Mother cooks acorn mush and deermeat stew as Wakara the Moon cooks them in her Sky Basket," he said in a low voice. Never before had he spoken words such as these at the wowi firepit. Elder Uncle nodded in agreement; Mother smiled her Yahi-bow smile in answer to them.

78

Said Grandfather, "Tck, tck, the wanasi eats like the First People. They knew only cold fire until one day an old woman stole a few coals of hot fire from the Fire People and brought them home hidden in her ear. Shaking them out of her ear into her firepit and adding wood and more wood, she cooked deermeat stew with stones heated in the hot fire. The First People ate of that stew till the basket was empty."

"So it is tonight in our wowi," said Mother. "We celebrate the return of our Young One, the Son."

Grandfather's words turned Ishi's thoughts to his journey. *Grandfather speaks truly; again the Yahi villages have only cold fire—all but Tuliyani. We seven are now the Fire People; we alone have Hot Fire.*

His thoughts came back to those around the firepit. *It is good to see Mother smile; to hear Grandmother and Tushi laugh. It is good to hear the mush say pukka pukka and to watch Tushi stir the stew with Mother's paddle. The smells of the wowi are good: dried fish and sweet herbs and the smell of the meadow in the tobacco which hangs over my head.*

The hair lies whiter on Grandfather's head and the creases deeper in his face. Grandmother's voice is more and more that of a bird. She is so skinny she looks like a bird when she swims in the creek. And she comes up the trail from the creek like a blackbird, hop, peck, hop, peck, stopping to laugh with Tushi or Grandfather.

I remember how Grandfather said to Mother many times in the winter, "You are a good daughter-in-law, My Younger Son's Wife." When his joints are swollen and he cannot sit or lie in comfort, Mother keeps him with her and puts warm poultices where the pain has entered his body. *All through the night she gives him fresh tea to drink and rubs the sore joints gently with oil from bay leaves.*

Grandmother says to her, "You make a baby of that old man. You spoil him so I can do nothing to suit him." Grandmother laughs when she says this, and touches Mother on the head with her hand. She looks to her as my Grandfather does, as we all do: without Mother, there would be no hot fire for us.

Timawi is not happy. Again he sits in the *watgurwa* through a whole day, or he goes where he can see the mountain. But his thoughts are not of the mountain. They are of himself, of Tushi.

Tushi is not with me as much as she used to be. She cannot go with me to hunt and she is often in her own small house talking with Grandmother, or she is there alone. Timawi and I sing songs outside her house when she stays for the night there. She pretends not to hear us, as Grandmother has taught her. Sometimes I see her when we go to the hills in the early dawn to pray or to gather wood for special fires. We pretend we do not see each other. This morning I was coming up the trail from the creek. I had gone swimming alone and I was shaking out my hair to dry it. There was Tushi beside the trail, and some of the water from my hair lay in drops on her face and throat. I put out my hand, touching her hair and her necklace where the water glistened, meaning to say I was sorry. She smiled, but then she ran back up the trail so fast I could not catch her.

Everyone in Tuliyani was busy with the tasks of late springtime. Elder Uncle and Ishi kept the drying frames full of salmon and deermeat. Grandfather and Grandmother went to the creek each day where Grandfather cast for trout and small fish. While he cleaned his catch, Grandmother sat stripping the black stems of five-finger ferns for new baskets.

One morning Elder Uncle asked Ishi to go below the alder tree crossing to count the beavers who lived in the marshes there. Beavers were trapped only when the marshes became crowded and a beaver family started to move downstream, out of the canyon, and beyond the reach of the Yahi.

Since Ishi would not be hunting—he would perhaps set a beaver trap—Mother said Tushi could go with him and gather brodiaea bulbs which grew thick on the hillside above the marshes.

They did not talk as they went through the brush, Tushi following behind Ishi. When they reached the marshes, and were sitting side by side, watching for the beavers, Tushi said, "For me, Sun traveled slowly above and below the earth while you were away, my Cousin."

"For me, too," Ishi replied. "But . . . . Timawi was with you in Tuliyani."

Tushi said nothing.

"Little Cousin, Timawi has told me he tried to give you a sweetgrass bracelet, but you would not take it."

Again there was a silence between them. The slap, slap of tails as two beavers added more mud to their dam was the only sound in the marshes.

"May I tell Timawi you will take it another time?"

Tushi shook her head.

"Timawi says you are dambusa like the young girl in Grandmother's story. . . . If you wore Timawi's bracelet he would not feel lonely in Tuliyani."

Tushi was trying not to cry. "Timawi wishes to leave Tuliyani—to take me with him to

Bushki, to be his Bushki-marimi. That is why I will not wear his bracelet. Did he tell you that?"

"No. He said nothing of wishing to leave, or of meaning to take you with him."

The tears could not be held. Tushi cried, covering her face with her hands, letting the rolls of hair fall over her face. "I shall never leave Grandmother or Mother or you!"

Ishi put his hand on Tushi's head. "Do not, O do not cry, Little Sister. I will talk to Timawi. I will go hunting with him to the mountain. When Timawi sees what the saldu have done to his village of Bushki he will not wish to take you there or to stay there himself. . . . Poor Tushi-White Shell! It is hard to be marimi, I know. It is hard to be wanasi!"

A Démon Doctor must have put a sickness on Timawi! He would not say such things to Tushi if he were well in his heart. He must not make her cry!

Tushi dried her eyes. Ishi went out on a log in the marsh to count how many beavers he could see in the dark water.

"Su, tetna!" It was Tushi's quick warning whisper. An old grizzly bear, his skin hanging loose on his ribs, was starting across the dam. He was drinking, and when fish came to the top of the water to feed, he tried to catch them. They were very small fish, so, over and over, his paw came out of the water, dripping, empty. At last he gave up and went away in the direction of the berry patch in Acorn Hollow.

Tushi dug brodiaea bulbs while Ishi made a bundle of some of the seasoned wood from the marsh. Tushi was still busy filling her basket when he had as much wood as he could carry. He kept a lookout while she worked, head down, thinking only of her digging. There were no sounds, no smells but familiar, earth smells; the world seemed empty except for the two of them. Ishi took his net and started uphill above Tushi to catch a butterfly for her. The large brilliantly colored butterfly he wanted kept out of his reach, fluttering up and up, leading him higher and higher toward the ridge. It lighted on a flower at last and Ishi crouched down by a rock to slip his net over it.

He heard nothing, but a smell of saldu and horse filled his nostrils. Without changing his position, he brought his bow around and took from his belt one of the three arrows stuck into it. He was well up toward the top of the ridge where the trail came from Acorn Hollow and the rock he crouched behind was between him and the trail. He took a quick look over the rock; what he saw filled his mouth with the salt water of fear.

Above him on the trail and outlined against the sky was a saldu on horseback. He had dropped his reins and was standing in his stirrups. In his hands was his lasso; he was making the first twist of the wrist which would set the rope in motion in a large flowing circle. His eyes were on Tushi; the rope was aimed to drop over her.

The inside of the twisting wrist showed white for an instant. There was the flash of a gleaming arrow in flight, a sharp yell of pain and the lasso dropped harmlessly to the ground; a second arrow flash, a snorting animal scream, and the horse, an arrow in his underbelly, reared, pawing the air. His hind feet slipped on the mud of the trail and he fell backwards, horse and rider going out of sight down the far side of the ridge.

Tushi was straightening up from her digging as Ishi grabbed her arm and pulled her along with him so fast her feet seemed not to touch the earth. They ran in this way until they came to the creek below Tuliyani. Tushi was crying from fright—Ishi's fright—she did not know who had screamed nor from what they were running. Ishi lay on his stomach now, sobbing. After awhile he crawled down the bank and dipped his head into the creek. Then he sat up, pushed his wet hair back, and told Tushi what had happened.

THE TALK went on late that night in the wowi and even later in the watgurwa. Said Elder Uncle, "Since seven turnings of the moons, our concealment from the enemy has been complete. This may bring them to the canyon; they will know some of us still live."

Timawi broke in, "You should have sent me to the beaver dam and to guard Tushi!"

Ishi turned his head away. *It hurts to hear Timawi speak in this way to my uncle. I am the cause of his doing so, and he speaks but the truth. . . . I see only that curving, circling rope, nearer, nearer.*

Grandfather spoke in anger. "Su! Does the Bushki-wanasi tell Kaltsuna how to make arrows?"

Elder Uncle shook a hand before his face, palm out. "The peace of seven moons is broken.

84

We are fearful and angry. We see again those three who were roped and dragged away. But let us not turn our anger and fear against each other in the watgurwa.

"To you, Timawi, I say look well into your heart before you speak further. And remember, the Little One sleeps, safe with Grandmother and Mother.

"You and Ishi and I will go together in the morning to see whether the saldu are gathering in Acorn Hollow as they did in the past when they were setting out to destroy one of the villages. We will go also to the beaver dam and there you can show the Young Hunter wherein he was at fault. He will learn from your greater skill and wisdom."

Timawi flushed and looked away and then back to Elder Uncle. Said Timawi, "I listen to the words of the Majapa. I will go with you as you say, to learn what we must know, not to teach or to boast."

It rained during the night; the Yuna Creek crossings were under white water and the rim trail was deep in mud. In the morning, Elder Uncle and the two wanasi went to the beaver dam, up the slope as Ishi had gone the day before, then on over the top of the ridge and part way down the other side.

There they found the horse, dead. Ishi took back his second arrow; he searched up and down the ridge for the one aimed at the twisting wrist of the rider. It was not on the trail or on the hillside below, nor did he ever find it.

The bridle was gone, but the saddle, blood and rain soaked, was still buckled around the horse. The rider had been alone: there were the tracks of the horse coming uphill and those of a man in riding boots going back downhill. Timawi and Ishi followed the tracks straight across Acorn Hollow. Neither going nor coming had there been any turning off to go to the saldu house in the hollow, nor did other tracks join these.

Timawi and Ishi dared not go farther. They were at the edge of the valley. But it was clear the saldu rider had left the hills without seeking help from those nearest at hand.

The three of them went to the rock behind which Ishi had crouched. Elder Uncle and Timawi both knew the difficulties of shooting uphill at a moving target. Elder Uncle said merely, "H'm'm. Su?" and looked at Timawi who said, "It is as well the butterfly led the Young Hunter to this rock where he did not have to change position to shoot."

They returned to Tuliyani. The rain stopped. No saldu came beating the brush for scalps and vengeance. The horse carcass was picked clean by mountain lions, coyotes and buzzards. The saddle, chewed by four-footers and dragged into the brush, was never reclaimed.

In the watgurwa, they wondered much about the man who had come and left so secretly. Said Grandfather, "That one must be without friends in his own world. There are saldu more alone than we in Tuliyani." But they no longer felt safe in Tuliyani. Many saldu were coming to the hills; they could hear the bleating of new-born lambs outside the canyon and it was time for the cows to calve.

Timawi urged Elder Uncle to move to Waganupa. He reminded him there were few saldu there and few saldu animals. Grandfather shook his head. "The People have never lived higher than Upper Meadow. The mountain gives shelter and food for only half the moons. There are no salmon there; the snow stays into summer and the winds blow each day."

Said Timawi, "Let Ishi and me go; we will look; perhaps we can find a cave or some other shelter from the winds. Here, we are caught as in a trap if the saldu find Tuliyani."

"Go then," said Elder Uncle. "I am no longer sure of what to do."

Timawi and Ishi left, expecting to be away five or six days. When they were gone, Grandfather said, "They are good wanasi; they hunt and shoot better than you and I, my son, when we were young. The Bushki-wanasi is heavier of build, heavier of thought than the Young One, but he is of great courage and skill. The Young One is quicker in the wrist motion with the bow and more understanding of the Way— or so I see him."

Tushi, in the brush behind Mother's house, waved to Timawi and Ishi as they left. She smiled at Timawi when he looked back, but it was Ishi she watched out of sight. To herself she said, "I will go to my little house tonight. There I will dream. In my dream Timawi, the Strong One, will offer me the sweetgrass bracelet. He will say, 'I will take you away from this canyon of flint. You will be my Bushki-marimi.'

"I will shake my head and put my hands behind my back. Then the Young Hunter will come, my cousin, tall, slim, his heavy hair coiled and piled high on his head, carved deerhorn ornaments in his nose and ears, the lion tail bow-cover hanging down his back. Running swift as a deer, he will take my hands and carry me, my feet skimming the earth, fast, far to the creek bank. There, lying straight and long, he will sob and sob. A man's tears are more terrible than a woman's, Grandmother says. Then he will bathe his head in the creek and turning, sit up and look at me with frightened eyes."

Grandmother found Tushi standing, looking

where the wanasi had gone from sight. "He is a handsome one, that Timawi, eh? The days and nights will be long while he is gone."

Tushi turned back to the wowi with Grandmother. "You will tell me tales of when you were young and the time will not be long." She held Grandmother's hand in one of hers; the other hand rested on the white and blue beads of her necklace.

ISHI and Timawi took only their bows and arrows, their hunting knives and slings, a fish net and a firedrill. They carried no food and no baskets. It was good to move without a load, to be out of the canyon, to smell the pines, to see Waganupa ever nearer.

They were well across Upper Meadow in time for their first sleep, a distance which would take three sleeps with the Old Ones. They raced each other. When they reached the top of a ridge, they went down the other side by jumping into a tree and sliding through the tree to the ground.

Timawi remembered a cave on the mountain. He also remembered some free-standing boulders, nearer than the cave, on the south slope. These might be even better as a living place, he and Ishi decided. Houses built between the rocks would be hidden, but would still look out to the mountain.

They fished in one of the little streams which poured from the melting snows of Waganupa.

The fish were small, "mountain fish," Timawi called them, "richer than the big fish below." They made a fire and when the fish were cooked and eaten, they talked about the new village: where its watgurwa would be, and Mother's house, and where Tushi would build her little house, and what they would call the village.

"I wonder—will Tushi wear my bracelet in the new village?"

"She will wear your bracelet if you do not try to take her from Grandmother and Mother."

"Or from you. She likes you better than she likes me."

Ishi touched his bow. *This is true and one must live by truth, Elder Uncle says.*

"Let there be peace between us, Timawi. You know well, Tushi is my cousin-sister. We had no playmate friends but each other in our childhood. There can be nothing between Tushi and me but the friendship of the firepit. We come from the same village, the same Old Ones.

"You—you are from far away—a Bushki. You eat mountain fish and marmots. There are words you say differently from the way they are said in the canyon. You look to the mountain. Tushi is your Dambusa One, from people who look to the water. You and Tushi should one day have an earth-covered house together."

"In Bushki, a woman went to the man's village."

"It does not have to be so. Father took Mother to Three Knolls only after I was born."

"The woman of Bushki goes with the man."

"Well . . . . we are few and Tushi is young. Let the moons turn once again over her little house."

There was no more talk that night. They saw smoke to the west, which meant there were saldu there. Ishi put out the fire and they made a shelter in the juniper at the edge of the meadow. But they did not sleep. Coyotes were howling and there was the constant barking of saldu sheep dogs. The late spring moon was full; it was very light there on the open meadow. There was also the bleating of sheep. Timawi crawled along the ground toward the nearest bleaters, coming back with two lambs.

"We vowed, after the giving of the bows, to eat no saldu food," Ishi said when he saw them.

"The saldu eat our food. That is an old vow. And a foolish one. Why should we not hunt saldu four-footers, as they hunt ours?"

"We will smell of sheep and saldu for the rest of this trip."

"There will be no time to hunt or fish tomorrow—it is better to have this food with us."

They were on their way ahead of Sun; and Sun was low in the west before they reached their second sleep place where they expected to make a fire and cook some of the sheep they had been carrying all day. The cluster of boulders was as Timawi had said; it looked to Ishi like a good place for a mountain village.

But no sooner had they found the place, than they picked up fresh spoor of bear, and as they came near, trying to stay downwind, a grizzly, followed by two cubs, came from behind the boulders. She got the smell of the sheep and with a growl, started downhill toward them. They did the only thing they could do—threw her the sheep, and ran. They ran until a juniper forest and two ridges and a stream were between them and the grizzly. On the far side of the stream, they stopped. They were on Bushki Creek and above Timawi's old village.

They had not eaten all day, nor could they risk making a fire: they were in country where saldu might be camping along the same creek with them. But Timawi was not hungry: he knew this stream; this was home!

"We could make a new Bushki village for all of us," he said.

"There are saldu in Bushki."

"And there are ways of making saldu go away. Grandfather did it; and your father. So can we."

My friend and I will quarrel if we go on with this talk. It has been a hard day; not like yesterday. "Grandmother says daylight is wiser than the dark. Let us sleep now and plan tomorrow."

Ishi fell into a deep but dream-crowded sleep. He tried to wake up, but went back into his dreams again. When he did at last waken enough to sit up, he was choking; the air was thick and heavy; he thought he heard distant thunder. There was a fire downstream. He could see the tops of tall pines blazing. He saw also above the smoke the star of the dawn shining in a clear sky; there had been no sky-fire, no thunder.

He spoke in a whisper to Timawi, but Timawi was no longer beside him. He felt for him in the dark, and crawled in wider and wider circles looking for him. He called, "Yagka yagka"—their call—Timawi was gone. There was no answer to his call.

Where would Timawi go without me? Why would he go? He might want to see his old home alone, to see if what I said was true—that the saldu built a house in the middle of the village.

Ishi followed the stream to Bushki, the smoke getting thicker the farther he went. Sun was up but pale through the smoke. The saldu storehouse was afire.

The thunder must have been from something which exploded inside the storehouse. Surely

Timawi is not here. Should I go back to our sleep place, or should I look for him below Bushki?

Undecided, Ishi shifted his feet, and touched a loose piece of wood; he could tell from the feel it was worked wood. He picked it up to look at it. It was Timawi's firedrill!

Ishi held it for some moments. *What is the meaning of its being here? Did Timawi set fire to the storehouse?*

Ishi put wet leaves over his face to keep from choking while he searched the ground. He found a bit of down and charcoal, enough to show him where Timawi could have made a fire; and close by were pine boughs dry enough for torches. *But if Timawi set fire to the house why did he not come back to where his drill lay?*

There was one footprint, then another. They were wide apart. *When a torch was lighted, he ran with it, leaping with wide-apart steps.*

Sun was past the top of the sky before Ishi found anything more, and this was on the lower side of the village: footprints of a horse and a dog. He smelled horse and sheep and sheep-dog. Then he found Timawi's sling, chewed by a four-footer and smelling of sheep-dog; and a short way from it, his tobacco pouch and his treasure bundle. They were chewed but the tobacco was there, and the treasure. Ishi took time to pick up everything he saw, and to rub out Timawi's and his own footprints.

He soon came to a place where the ground was stirred up. Here there were a few drops of blood, and four of Timawi's arrows lay scattered. *Here the dog must have attacked him; I think that is dog blood because there are dog hairs; Timawi must have used his knife. Here are Timawi's footprints; here the dog's; and*

*again Timawi's, going off toward the first bluff
of the canyon!*

Ishi did not wait; he ran where Timawi had
run, and jumped down the bluff as he was sure
Timawi had done, into the top of an oak tree
which broke the speed of his jump. He slid
safely to the ground. Timawi lay close to the
foot of the oak tree. He looked unhurt; Ishi spoke
to him. His eyes were closed as if he slept. He
did not move.

*Perhaps his soul has left his body; it will
return when he wakens; I will not disturb him.*

Ishi went to the other side of his sleeping
friend. "Aii-ya! Here is blood! My friend, my
friend, speak to me!" Ishi lifted Timawi's head,
turned him over. "Aahh! You will not speak!
There is the smoke mark where a fireball hit
you—at the moment of jumping, O Timawi!"

*But there were no saldu footprints in Bushki
—ahh! The horse! A dog and a saldu on horseback!* Ishi lay, both arms across Timawi, crying.
Everything blurred before his eyes and he did
not know what he did.

Sun was long since gone; the full moon made
the world as bright as day. Ishi stumbled and
fell. He came back to himself then. He saw
that much time had gone by, that it was night,
and that he was no longer under the oak tree.
He was on the trail down Banya Canyon, carrying Timawi.

He stood up, settled Timawi on his back as he
must have been before he fell, and walked on
again. A coyote bayed nearby; a mountain lion
crossed the trail ahead of him, a rabbit in its
mouth; deer moved wakefully in the brush. He
passed a rattlesnake, coiled and awake in the
middle of the night.

*What do I do here, and where is it I go? There
are no saldu in this canyon—the saldu did not*

know that my friend jumped—or did not dare follow him. I feel safe, and as if my feet know where to go.

In this waking-dreaming state, Ishi went on. The moon was gone and dawn had come, and Ishi was at Ancestor Cave. Only then did he know this was where his feet were taking him. He went inside the cave, brushing off the smooth stone slab which he remembered from his journey. Gently, he brought his friend there, laid him on the clean stone, and rolled rocks across the entrance of the cave so no four-footer could come in.

There, alone, Ishi performed the burial rites as he had learned them in the watgurwa—he had never seen them. When the fire and the tobacco and pine resin which he threw on the fire were turned to ash and were cold, he lifted the slab to one side, laid his friend in the rock-lined burial place with the Ancestors, and put the stone slab back in place. Ishi worked in darkness much of the time.

He kept no count of days or nights, nor did he eat or sleep. It was night when he left the cave, replaced the boulders in the cave entrance for the last time, and started home. He bathed in the creek above Black Rock before going down the trail toward Tuliyani. It was then early morning.

TO THOSE in Tuliyani the days after Timawi
and Ishi left were long, each longer and more
anxious than the one before. Sun rose over
Waganupa and went under the western edge of
the earth seven, eight times.

Tushi went in the brush close to the trail as
far as Mother would allow, looking and listening for the absent wanasi. It was the morning
of the ninth sunrise. Tushi was almost at Black
Rock when she heard the soft beat of bare,
running feet on the earth. Ishi and Timawi
must be coming down the trail from the three
knolls! She waited, and in a short time, a
single head appeared briefly through an opening in the chaparral—it was Ishi.

Briefly—but long enough for Tushi to see
he was alone. She put a hand over her mouth
and made no sound. Ishi's long brush of hair
was gone, burned off close to his head, meaning
someone dear to him had died, and across his
face were painted the wide black stripes of
mourning.

Tushi ran and caught up with him but she
said no word, waiting for him to speak. He said
only, "Our uncle?" Tushi pointed to the creek.
"Fishing," she said. Ishi motioned her to go
home. She watched him out of sight, then turned
toward Tuliyani.

Ishi took the trail to the creek. Elder Uncle
was there preparing to fish. His words of greet-

ing dried on his lips. "Where is our friend?" he asked.

"In Banya canyon; in Ancestor Cave."

"And the—his Spirit?"

"All has been done that I could do. His Spirit is released. He lies with the Ancestors. I have bathed and said the purification prayer."

Elder Uncle's hands shook so that he found it hard to take his pouch from his belt. From the flat palm, he blew a pinch of the sacred tobacco over Ishi, repeating the prayers which would protect him from any danger remaining with him from his closeness to the Spirit World.

Then, one after another, he blew five pinches of the sacred tobacco to the west where he knew Timawi's Spirit would be journeying to the Land of the Dead; and he repeated the prayers for the Dead. Only when this was done, and his pouch put away again, did Elder Uncle say, "Sit down. Tell me—from the beginning."

At the end of the telling, Ishi said, "When my soul returned to my body and I saw I was in the canyon, I was not afraid. The Ancestor-Spirits must have come to me at the foot of the oak tree; perhaps they smelled the burning pines. It seems to me I did as they wished me to do. I made the fire over the burial place and said the prayers Grandfather taught me, and made sure the wanasi's bow and arrows, his pouch and treasure bundle and some acorn meal were beside him for his journey. But I may not have done all as it should be done. Perhaps it was wrong to go to Ancestor Cave. . . . It is not easy to be wise alone."

Ishi rubbed his hand over his face. His eyes were bloodshot; he was drawn, pale and thin. Elder Uncle was crying now, not trying to hide his tears. "You were wise beyond the moons of your life, my Son. I should not have let our friend go to the mountain, but it seemed the canyon could no longer hold him. Soon he will be at the campfire of his people from Bushki. There will be bears to fight in the Land of the Dead; mountains, and tall pine trees; and those who taught him to shoot and to jump when he was a boy.

"We mourn for ourselves, Younger Brother's Son, for what you and I shall do without him, I do not see. . . . But go you, now, go to Mother and her food basket. You have not eaten since six suns and more. Nor slept. Eat some of Mother's good acorn mush. Tonight you will sleep. You must let your heart lighten a little."

Those in Tuliyani mourned for Timawi. They never again spoke his name, calling him instead "Our Friend," or "The Restless One." Ishi was made to tell over and over all that happened at Bushki. Grandfather said, "Our friend was brave; he might not have been caught so easily except for the smell of sheep which brought the dog."

It was Tushi who first changed this talk to recalling the Restless One as he was in life. Soon the others spoke no more of his death but of him as the Bushki hunter of elk, the strong swimmer, the one who liked to lie awake all night in the summer telling hunting stories.

Ishi did not see Tushi crying, but he was sure she did cry, alone, in her little house. One day he motioned her to come with him. She followed him to the creek where they sat side by side on a bank of young clover. Tushi had not spoken all the way; she kept her face turned away; Ishi saw her wipe the back of her hand across her eyes.

"Do not cry, Little Cousin—or if you must, can you tell me why you cry?"

"It is the Bushki-hunter. . . . I wish, O I wish I had let him give me his sweetgrass bracelet!"

"Here it is." Ishi opened his pouch. "He carried it in his treasure bundle. I did not put it with the other treasures to go with him because I knew he would want you to have it. I've been waiting to give it to you. Take it, Little White Shell." Ishi held it out to her. "Wear it."

"No, O, no!"

"It is yours. We talked—the Restless One and I—about you and him. I told him you would one day be his Bushki-marimi. I said to him, 'Tushi will wear your bracelet. Only wait a few moons.'"

"Aiku tsub! I will put it with my treasures."

"Wear it, Tushi."

"No, I shall never wear it."

"Why should you not? It was meant that you and our friend should one day have an earth-covered house together."

Tushi gave Ishi a strange look, as though she were older than he, as old as Mother, as old as Grandmother.

"That is the dreaming of the Old Ones. My dream is different and has not to do with this empty world. We are not Heroes or Gods; this is not the beginning of things; we cannot make People to fill the emptiness, to fight the saldu."

"Suwa, White Shell Girl! But—what is this dream you speak of?"

"It is a woman's dream."

"Is it forbidden to tell it to a man?"

"It is not forbidden. I will tell it to you, because you gave me the white shell name, and my dream, too, is white."

And there on their mat of green clover in the spring sunshine Tushi told Ishi her White Dream.

"My dream begins in greenness, like the green clover here. Everything looks as when I am awake. Then—I go across to the other side of the creek—it could be right here. On the other side, the rocks and ground and bushes are moss-covered, soft, still. I turn to the north, and as I go farther, always north, the green softness changes to white. Everything is white and soft and still. Far, far from home, I come to a house. Someone inside the house calls to me to come in.

"The house is larger than any I have known before; like the houses Grandmother tells of, when there were many People. This house is so big, I enter it by way of the covered passageway meant for young children, yet I do not have to bend or crawl, but I walk, straight, through it. Inside, an old man and an old woman are sitting. Their hair is white. Everything is white. The house is made of ice, the seats the two Old Ones sit on are of ice. The firepit is white and ice-covered. Even the eyelashes of the man and woman are white.

"I think at first the Old Ones must be made of rock, but the woman speaks. She says, 'Go to your mother. See, she sits there.' And there truly is my mother! She puts her arms around

99

me and holds me close to her. She says, 'Come, My Daughter, eat. You must be hungry after your long journey.' I eat. This makes her smile, and the food tastes good even though it is ice.

"My older sister is there. I think all of my family is there, behind my mother, if I could see them. My mother says, and my sister, 'This is a good place; there are flowers and green grass. We are happy here.'

"Then the house is gone. I am outside again and the old man calls to me, saying it is time to go home.

"I am not cold in all that ice. And my mother and my sister are not cold. I do not see the flowers and the grass, but my mother sees them. . . . I believe it is a good dream."

"I believe, too, it is a good dream," said Ishi when Tushi was finished.

This may be a Power Dream. White Shell Woman lives in Outer Ocean. She could give Tushi a Power Dream.

BUT CLOSER than dreams was the enemy. The Restless One had been right; they must move from Tuliyani. Where? Not to the mountain; not lower in the canyon; where?

For four days Ishi was gone from dawn to dusk, and the fifth day and night as well. When he returned, and he and Elder Uncle and Grandfather were in the watgurwa, his uncle said, "Has the wanasi found secret treasure? Some of Kaltsuna's striped flint or the blue-glass rock?"

Ishi smiled. "The wanasi has found no treasure which can be brought to Tuliyani. He has found a hidden place for us to live—a bear's den."

"A bear's den! My Brother spoke truly when he gave you the name of Tehna, Cub-Bear."

"Will you come with me to see it?"

"I will if you wish it, although my days of hunting bear are over."

"And Mother, will she come?"

"Su! I do not think Mother wishes to share a bear's firepit."

Tushi persuaded Mother; so it was that Elder Uncle and Mother, Ishi and Tushi went for a trip of five sleeps to see Ishi's bear-den, leaving Grandmother and Grandfather at home.

They traveled under cover of trees and brush. No saldu, riding the ridge trail or fishing in Yuna Creek, heard so much as a footfall as, hour after hot hour, the four of them worked their way up out of the canyon, around the three knolls and over the ridge into Banya Creek Canyon. It was roundabout, not the way Ishi went when he was alone, but it was the safest way over the high ridge which separated the two canyons.

They slept under trees the first night at the top of the ridge, and the second night on Badger Creek, which flowed into Banya Creek. The next day was the hardest, because, although the distance was short, they had to crawl through brush so heavy that each bush, each clump, was a thorny barrier blocking their slow way. It was very hot and there was no water. The day's trip was from the rim to less than halfway down the canyon wall to a narrow ledge.

101

On the ledge was the bear's den—a wide-mouthed cave at the base of a cliff which rose sheer and bare to the top of the canyon. Nothing of the cave could be seen until they were upon it. Ishi had found it by chance; it was completely overgrown with poison oak, except for the top of the arching roof, which had made him think of Green Cave.

There hung in the air of the cave a faint smell of grizzly bear, like the bear rug in Tuliyani when it was damp. Although long empty, there was no doubt it had once been, as Elder Uncle said, Wowunupo-mu-tetna: Grizzly Bear's Hiding Place.

The high roof overhung the lip of the cave; inside, the floor was level for the length of Mother's house, then sloped upward, narrowing at the back in a series of steps or shelves of rock.

Ishi had described the cave to Tushi: as soon as she saw it, she wished to live there. And Mother smiled her slow Yahi-bow smile, saying only, "I like it." It was back in the country of her young days. She could not see Gahma, but she knew it was directly below, at the bottom of the canyon. She could imagine the rock shelves filled with baskets of all sizes; she saw that the smooth rock would be dry and easy to keep brushed and clean. There was room for everyone to sleep in the cave in the time of rain and snow moons. Ishi drew a circle where Mother said the firepit should be.

Elder Uncle did not much take to the idea of living in a bear's den: no Yahi had ever done so! But, Wowunupo-mu-tetna was a place no saldu animal would risk legs or horns to reach, and it would not be in a saldu's mind that a village could be set on the straight-up-

and-down-wall of a canyon. He was not sure it was in his own mind that it could.

They ate the acorn bread and dried fish Mother and Tushi brought from home, and drank the water Ishi carried in a basket from Badger Creek. Said Elder Uncle, "We might come to Wowunupo before the end of the next Harvest Moons—what do you think, Mother of Tehna-Ishi?"

"I think it would be good to celebrate the Harvest Feast in Wowunupo," was Mother's answer. Tushi and Ishi smiled at each other. "We shall make a village such that Flint Man himself could live here," said Ishi to Tushi, who answered, "I shall carry hot fire in my ear from Tuliyani for the New Fire of Wowunupo!"

They returned to Tuliyani as they had come, sleeping again at Badger Creek and under the trees. There was nothing to eat the last day but some chokecherries they picked on the way. Back in Tuliyani, Grandfather had caught trout, and while they cooked the fish on green sticks in front of the fire, they told Grandfather and Grandmother of all they had seen and done, and of the new home, Wowunupo-mu-tetna, which Ishi had found for them.

Ishi and Tushi, who did most of the moving from Tuliyani to Wowunupo, made many trips back and forth over the steep short way Ishi had found between the two villages. Ishi carried the heavy stone mortars and the largest baskets. Food, blankets, tools, treasure bundles, all must go. Tushi came only to Ishi's shoulder and she was slim with small hands and feet, like Mother, but, like Mother, she was strong and she knew how to carry a load on her back, swung from a head-strap of deerskin, which left her hands free. And over many moons, she had learned to keep up with Ishi at whatever pace he went.

Grandmother said, "No Yahi woman ever did such work!"

Tushi laughed. "It is you, Grandmother, who taught me a Yahi woman does what is to be done."

"I did not teach you to go through brush at night with a load on your back; or to go alone with your own cousin."

Mother and Elder Uncle let Grandmother talk, and they let Tushi go with Ishi. Said Mother to Elder Uncle, "It is as well Grandmother tells Tushi how it was in the Old Days. . . . Tushi is like a young pine tree—she grows in the shade of larger trees; and, like the pine, she, too, stands alone, with a little space around her."

Elder Uncle nodded. "Yes, such is the Little One since the Hunter from Bushki is gone."

The moving was completed. Ishi put earth over the cold ashes of the wowi and watgurwa firepits. Elder Uncle blew smoke from his pipe over the empty village. From this time, Tuliyani was no longer for living Yahi—it belonged to the Ancestors.

Said Elder Uncle:

Suwa!
May the footmarks and handmarks
Of the People
All up and down the canyon
Over the hills
And in the meadows

Go under the earth
Leaving no sign or memory
On rock or tree or stream.

May all things be as they were
Before Jupka made the People.

And Elder Uncle said:

> Suwa!
> May the brush grow rank and tall
> Swallowing the villages
> Catching the clumsy feet
> Of the saldu and their four-footers
> Throwing them to the earth.
>
> Soon the enemy
> With his destroying weapons
> Shall be as nothing here.
>
> The canyon has already forgotten him.
> Suwa!

Grandfather, Grandmother, Elder Uncle, Mother, Ishi and Tushi turned from Tuliyani and Yuna Canyon to Banya Canyon, to Wowunupo. Nor did they turn back to look a last time, to cry, to waken the sad and happy memories of all they were leaving.

The trip to Wowunupo with the Old Ones was slow and dangerous. Elder Uncle went ahead, making sure they were not coming on a party of saldu; there were saldu and saldu four-footers at every turn, it seemed to Grandfather. Ishi and Tushi knew the good resting places along the way; they made little brush shelters where the Old Ones could sleep; and Tushi always remembered to have a basket of fresh water waiting for them.

Like the other trips to Wowunupo, this one with the Old Ones was made without any saldu knowing of it. The last day through the brush down to the ledge, Ishi stayed only a step ahead, bending back branches, cutting or pulling aside brambles. They were scratched, thirsty and cramped from the long hours of crawling, but when they saw Wowunupo, the Old Ones forgot their weariness.

"We are Ancestors in truth," said Grandfather, sitting down in the cave. "We are Flint Man and Flint Woman. We live in a House of Flint. For capes, we will powder ourselves with flint dust as Kaltsuna did. Aiku tsub." And if it was too steep and too far to the creek for those Old Ones to go to swim as they were accustomed to do, they never spoke of it. They washed their mouths, faces and bodies each day, using only the basket of fresh water Ishi or Tushi brought them in the morning. They were as busy as the others making Wowunupo a place for people, not a bear's hiding place.

The cave became the family house, the wowi, with an earth-covered addition which partly closed the entrance. Ishi made this strong and tight, using strips of cedar bark to bind the frame together. In the winter, there would be only a narrow opening which could be closed with a deerskin flap, tied from the inside.

Elder Uncle and Ishi built a storage house, a covered drying and smoking shelter, and a watgurwa, with barely room to hold Elder Uncle, Grandfather and Ishi. The watgurwa was well downstream from the cave, and the ledge was not cleared of its trees and brush, so that each little house stood alone, hidden, with only the faintest of trails leading around the trees from one to another.

Close to the storage house there grew a tall gray pine; its long needles were outlined against the sky; its large cones were filled with nuts. This pine was a landmark, standing higher than the surrounding trees. Ishi cleared a circle of ground under the pine as the village center.

There was no water in Wowunupo. Rainwater could be caught in baskets; and in the early spring there would be little, close-by, freshets of water, but for the long moons of late spring, summer and fall, all water would have to be carried from Banya Creek in baskets, up the steep rough trails. Ishi measured and marked out a space under the pine tree in the shade, one bow-length by two in size. Then he dug it to the depth of two bow-lengths. This would be a place to pack winter snow and so save many trips to the frozen creek. When Elder Uncle saw what he was doing, he helped him pack and tamp the heavy adobe soil, making it smooth and almost watertight.

Mother and Tushi made a tiny woman's shelter close to the cave-wowi; it held only one of them at a time. They stored their dyes and ferns and feathers for their fine baskets on the highest shelves at the back of the cave; and there they kept also their treasure bundles.

Beyond the watgurwa, the ledge was already shallower, and Ishi set up a bark canopy over a natural hollow, where he made a cache of flint and obsidian. Within a few days, slivers and chips from rock-glass began to pile up there, for Ishi was at work. This was the end of the village and the ledge also came to an end ten bow-lengths farther downstream.

The trails into Wowunupo were straggly and narrow, no more than the runways of foxes and badgers; and they were kept so. From the gray pine, and going down over the ledge to the creek, was a faint trail which had been made by the bears which used to live in Wowunupo. Ishi named it the Tetna Trail and it, too, was kept as it was. Tetna Trail was under cover of brush all the way. It ended at the top of the creek bank which was very steep; and there, Ishi hid a rope in the brush by which he swung himself down to the water. It was not easy to climb back up the steep face of the bank with a filled basket hung from a head-strap, but he learned to do it, clinging to the rope with feet and hands.

Between Gahma, upstream, and the end of the tetna trail, a tall alder grew over the water at a steep angle, its roots half-exposed. Working with wedges and ropes, Elder Uncle and Ishi further loosened the roots, until they were able, by pulling and by lying as heavily as they could against the trunk of the tree, to make it fall across Banya Creek, the top coming to rest on the farther bank.

"Aiiya! Now we have an alder log crossing, like the one on Yuna Creek." Elder Uncle was pleased.

"But this is much higher. . . ." Tushi looked fearfully down at the creek from the log. Gone was the quiet, dark pool of Gahma; here, the water roared and foamed over huge boulders.

"There is no other way," Elder Uncle told Tushi. "The banks are higher here. Also, Banya Creek is deeper than Yuna Creek. A lower crossing would be carried away during flood-time."

Leafy treetops formed a complete canopy over the village of Wowunupo. The cave roof blackened from Mother's fires, but it kept the smoke a secret from any outsider. Instead of rising in a blue coil, it seeped and floated out of the cave and among the bushes like a drifting bit of Kaltsuna's blue-flint dust.

UNTIL the watgurwa was finished, the firepit dug and the cave itself made tight for winter, Ishi had time and thought for nothing else. Now, these tasks were finished and the baskets were full. He went to his workplace in the hollow at the end of the ledge. He started to flake a spear point, but he soon put his flaker down.

Now all is done. The Old Ones again laugh and sing by the fire; Mother says it is a good village. . . . Aii-ya! Wowunupo closes in on me today as Yuna Canyon pressed in upon the Restless One. . . . Since the morning he and I left Tuliyani together, I have not sung with my bow nor listened for the Monster. And here, there is no Black Rock!

Ishi turned uphill from the hollow. A short

scramble through brush brought him to a patch of shale rock. Across the shale, he climbed steeply through a stand of madrone and gray pine to a bluff which overhung the canyon. He had seen this bluff from a distance but had never been out on it. Now he went to the edge and was surprised to discover that he could see down-canyon to a wedge-shaped opening onto the Great Valley.

Su! A Lookout Point for Wowunupo! It is nearer to the village than is Black Rock to Tuli-yani; and nearer the Monster. There will be only a glimpse of his smoky head from here, but I should hear him plainly.

Sun traveled down and down the Sky Road to the west. The Great Valley and the sky glowed with the end-of-day reds and purples of Sun's headdress; the River Daha became a rope of curving fire. The Monster appeared briefly in the sunset glow, its Whu-HOOH-huu louder than from Black Rock, its smoke pink against the red sky as it followed the river around a bend and out of sight.

Ishi put an offering of tobacco on a rock, and left Lookout Point only when the last of the color was gone and the first stars began to glow in the Sky World. *For the first time in many moons, my Dream again seems near to me. I had thought I no longer knew how to dream.*

Said Elder Uncle to Grandfather and Ishi in the watgurwa a few nights later, "The moons bring rain early. Let us go, Younger Brother's Son, you and I, to hunt on the mountain. The baskets are full, to be sure, but the New Year and the green clover may be slow in coming and winter may lie long in Wowunupo."

Ishi remembered this trip with Elder Uncle all his life. They were gone for the space of more than half a moon; the days were the low-sun days of harvest time, the nights bright with the harvest moon. They spoke, the two of them, as one man to another. And during the whole of the hunt, they were free of saldu, who had left the meadows to hunt on the far side of the mountain. Elder Uncle and Ishi made their camp close to Upper Meadow, and from there went to the top of Waganupa.

Ishi told Elder Uncle of his journey through the Yahi World; and he showed him where he and the Restless One had gone, and told him of what they talked. Elder Uncle spoke of himself as a young wanasi; and of his dreams. He told Ishi of the wife he had lost when Bay Tree Village was overrun; and something of what he had meant his life to be before the saldu put an end to that old life.

Surely this uncle was meant to be the head of a family, the Majapa of a village, like those great Majapas whose names and deeds Grandfather has related to me. Elder Uncle must feel pressed in by Wowunupo, by all of life sometimes. He says nothing of this; he does not forget or deny the Way.

The hunting was good; there were deer, ducks and gray geese feeding in the meadow, and a herd of elk. The elk paid no attention to Ishi and Elder Uncle, who spent much time listening to their call and learning to imitate it; they watched how the leader walked, with the female and young buck elk following behind; how sometimes the young bucks fought with each other and sometimes challenged the leader. "But," said Elder Uncle, "that Old One is still a better fighter and smarter than the young ones. If they lose him, none of them is ready to lead the herd."

They shot one of the young bucks, which gave them much good meat and hide and antler and

111

bone. When they started home, they left caches along the way which Ishi would bring in to Wowunupo as he could.

Elder Uncle understood the signs of an early winter and a long one. The green clover moon was slow in coming, but Wowunupo-mu-tetna was warm and dry, and with the extra baskets of food from the mountain hunt, those in the cave were kept from hunger until the spring salmon at last came up Banya Creek.

For one and then another turning of the moons of the seasons all was well with the People of Wowunupo. The two Old Ones moved from the cave to the sunny cleared space around the gray pine in the center of the village, wrapped in their capes and blankets when it was cold. They spoke of themselves as "Ancestors," and they were in very truth more and more like Ancestors. They sat, while Sun went from high to low across the Sky World, looking to the west, Grandfather holding Grandmother's little claw of a hand in his own not-so-much-larger hand.

Grandfather was never sick, but he was stiff and no longer strong. Pains had entered his joints, and there was no Kuwi, no Doctor, to suck them out. They caused swellings, and made any movement difficult and painful. When spring came for the second time in Wowunupo, he did not go anymore to the watgurwa and Mother could see he would be leaving them soon. It was his great age which was turning his eyes and thoughts to the west.

He said to Mother, "The journey to Wowunupo was my last but one. I am too old to go anywhere but down the Trail."

Before the moons brought the fierce heat of summer to the canyon, Grandfather was gone.

Grandmother did not cry much, but each sunrise after Grandfather's going, it was harder and harder for her to breathe. "The air grows heavier and heavier," she said. "I can no longer lift it to my mouth. I need the old Kuwi to fan up a lighter air."

Tushi tried to fan up a lighter air, and she made trip after trip through the heat to bring fresh water with cool berries crushed in it, because Grandmother ate nothing at all.

When Mother came with a basket of tea for her, Grandmother saw she had been crying. She put her hand on Mother's head in the old way. "Do not cry for the Ancestors, my Daughter. It is not you or Tushi who need me now; it is that Old One who forgot to wait for me. I wish only to follow down the Trail after him. We were so long together, I cannot remember how to live apart from him."

Before the third harvest in Wowunupo, Grandmother had followed Grandfather to the Land of the Dead.

Tushi cried when Grandmother was gone. She turned to Mother; but Mother could only cry with her. Tears ran down Elder Uncle's face. Ishi took his bow to the hollow where he cried alone, thinking sometimes of the Old

Ones, but thinking also of Elder Uncle's grief and of Tushi's and Mother's tears. *Aa-hh! The tears of my People! My Mother's tears! Only once before have I seen her cry this way!*

When Ishi returned to the cave, Elder Uncle was saying to Mother, "We must help our Little One to live. The Old Woman, her thoughts much in the past, talked of the Old Days and so gave her own past to the Young One. Now Tushi has only her memory of the Old One's memories to live by. It is not enough. You, Mother, must pray to White Shell Woman; she has much power and her dreams are healing dreams."

Ishi saw how Mother dried her tears and how she and Elder Uncle put away their grief; how they kept the circle around the fire so that each looked into the faces of the others and the four did not huddle together; how they talked sometimes in the fashion of the Old Ones so the talk around the fire was not without stories and the little jokes of the Old Ones; how they spoke often of them as they were in life, until Ishi and even Tushi learned to speak of them and think of them without crying.

Ishi went to Lookout Point for the first time since the Old Ones were gone. He sat looking out over the canyon, and into the wedge of the Great Valley.

To lose the Old Ones is hard, very hard. They were Ancestors, as they said, in life as in death. Long before their time, came the First People— the Beginners. Now, after their time, no others come. There remain only four—a Mother, an Uncle, and two Cousins. These are the People who must live without Young or Old, without hope—the Ending, the Last People. Jupka made this World for the People; but Jupka turned himself into a butterfly long, long before the enemy came here: he knew nothing of the no-color saldu.

Ishi lay down, looking through half-closed eyes into the low-slanting plumes of Sun's headdress. A jupka butterfly fluttered before his eyes, its wings taking on the colors of the sunset.

It is late in the day for a jupka. Winter will soon be here, when only the white cocoon houses of the butterflies are to be seen.

The Monster's voice came to Ishi from the Valley; in the still air it sounded near and familiar and friendly. He did not sit up to look at it; he was already half-asleep. When it was gone around a bend, he slept and as he slept he dreamed.

In his dream he traveled into the sunset, becoming part of it, moving without effort down the River Daha, brilliant as a flaming rope, and on to the gathering of waters where the rivers flow together. And so he came to the Edge of the World.

There it was as Grandfather had told him long ago: Sun plunged under the edge of the world into Outer Ocean, causing the ocean to boil up over the land, sending waves far up the shore. The waves flowed back again, leaving shells, white and purple, on the shore. *These are gifts from White Shell Woman whose home is in Outer Ocean.*

In the dream, Ishi, too, plunged into Outer Ocean, following Sun across the underside of the World from west to east, a trip which took all night. Of this trip, Grandfather had said, "When the earth was flat and empty, Jupka the God turned it upside down and made a straight, broad road across its underside from west to east, then turned it right side up again. This is the road Sun travels at night when it is dark."

It was just as Grandfather said, and in the

morning, Sun climbed back over the eastern edge onto the earth, the long plumes of his headdress streaming up, up until the earth and sky were all alight. Then he began once again his day-trip over the Sky Road above the earth from east to west.

Ishi opened his eyes. He was on Lookout Point, lying as when he went to sleep in the sunset. It was morning; the Monster called Whu-HOOH-huu from the Valley, and the jupka butterfly of the night before clung to a warm rock beside Ishi, its wings frail against the morning wind.

Ishi lay still for a little longer. Sun shone warm on him; he wanted to think about his dream. *My Dream is never the same. But its road is surely Sun's road. And this time, the Monster came at its beginning and at the end.*

Ishi stood up. He lifted his arms up, up, stretching toward Sun. *Suwa! It is good to dream! . . . . My Dream gives me courage. Sun shines. My bow is beside me. Below in Wowunupo are my Mother, my Uncle, and Little White Shell, my Cousin. Aiku tsub!*

3

THE ENDING PEOPLE

THE MOONS of the changing seasons grew from crescents to full and became old and pale many, many times. When the Five Sisters of the Sky World danced over Ishi's head he knew it was midwinter, and he carved a notch in the handle of his harpoon. The notches were five to a tier. Four tiers were filled and a fifth begun since the first harvest feast in Wowunupo.

Tushi ran her fingers down the harpoon handle, counting. "More than twice ten moon-seasons are marked here! You and I are no longer young, wanasi. We have learned well the life of the cave, of hiding, su?"

"Yes, Little White Shell, we, the Ending People."

The cousins looked at each other and smiled.

She may no longer be young in moons, but my Cousin is to me as she has always been. Her cheeks keep the toyon berry color; her hair is smooth and shining as when Grandmother rolled it for her; she walks straight and light of foot as is the way of Yahi women; her voice is soft as the quail—sigaga sigaga she calls to me.

Since many moons we go together when we are away from Wowunupo. If I hunt, she goes over the hill and does a woman's task until the kill is made. We gather acorns together and firewood, and we plan together each day where we shall go; what we shall do. She fills the moons of my days.

To herself, Tushi said, "My Cousin, the wanasi, looks as he looked when he first put his hair up in the old way of the Yahi Hunter. I have followed him since I could run; always I wait for him to call; then I come. My days are full of him, nor do I dream my White Dream any more."

Ishi no longer went often to Lookout Point to see the Monster, and his Dream, too, was far from him. Ishi and Tushi lived the life of the cave, as Tushi said. They thought of the enemy only to be careful to avoid him.

They knew there were more and more cattle and horses and sheep in the Yahi hills, and more saldu cabins. There were saldu living on lower Yuna Creek and they had seen a sawmill built in Acorn Hollow. They knew by smell, by the echo of a strange voice, by the sharp striking of a shod hoof on a rock, when a pack train was coming. They paced its course to a cabin where they saw the horse feed, the sacks of flour and coffee and the slabs of salted meat unloaded and placed on shelves. They stayed close to the pack train until it left the hills.

Saldu miners, looking for the bright rocks and dust in the creeks, traveling alone with a horse or a burro, dug and panned for a season during the heat moons, and left, not knowing that a Yahi man and a Yahi woman watched all they did.

Saldu came once with picks and shovels and began to widen the trail down the canyon. Ishi and Tushi smiled when they saw the saldu, instead, change the course of the trail so that it crossed Banya Creek higher up where the brush was less dense, and went south, out of the Yahi World.

"It was Grandfather who caused the first saldu to go south, away from the canyons," said Ishi.

No saldu hunters or miners or fishermen and no saldu four-footers, during all those moons, came into the heavy brush surrounding Wowunupo.

When they were away from the village, Tushi usually stepped in Ishi's footprints. While Ishi watched out for what might be ahead, Tushi made sure no frazzled bit of rope or string was left behind to show where they had been. Ishi never dropped an arrowhead or a feather, and Tushi let nothing fall from her baskets. When it rained, their footsteps went deep into the mud. Then they stopped to fill such prints with rock and to cover the rock with leaves.

Where they could, they jumped from rock to rock, from boulder to boulder, so no mark was left behind. And they swam for long distances underwater, or walked in the water where it was shallow and protected by overhanging willows. The water held no mark of their having been there, and they moved as silently through the water as on land.

A little at a time, they had cleared and cut tunnels through the brush, barely high and wide enough to crawl through. In this way they came and went without wearing trails into Wowu-nupo, or to Tushi's favorite berry patches or to the creek or any other places where they went often.

Sometimes, Ishi climbed the gray pine in the center of Wowunupo. From the tree he could see the creek at the bottom of the canyon and a piece of the rim overhead. He could also hear much better than within the brush-screen which enclosed the village. He picked the huge cones before they dropped or the squirrels got to them. They were full of fat pine nuts which he and Tushi shook out, putting the cones aside for the fire when they were empty.

While Ishi was up in the gray pine, Tushi lay in the cleared circle beneath it, looking at the sky between the dark branches and long spreading needles. One day, she called to Ishi, "Come down, Wanasi-cousin. I think this tree is the Sky Pole. If you go to visit the Sky People, I want to go, too."

They talked of the Sky People when whistling

swans and gray geese and ducks alighted on the meadows and then flew off toward the sky. They knew that these high-flying birds flew easily through the opening where the Sky Pole pierced the sky. Tushi wondered what the Sky People were like.

"Sky People used to come to the earth to visit," said Ishi, "but I think, with the enemy everywhere, the Pole has been drawn up into the Sky World. Grandfather said it was close to the foot of Waganupa, but Elder Uncle does not remember where, and I have looked for it many times, but I have never seen it."

When not hunting, fishing and gathering, they sat around Mother's firepit in the cave, or outside under the gray pine. They retold the tales Grandmother and Grandfather used to tell; they sang the old songs and sometimes they danced. Ever more closely encircled by the enemy saldu and their animals, the four people, Mother, Elder Uncle, Ishi and Tushi lived, hidden, watchful, and unknown to the nearest saldu or to any saldu. And the pattern of their lives did not change.

Mother, who all her life had run up and down the house ladder and the steep canyon trails as if she were a young girl, got a sickness, a bad sickness which caused her ankles to swell and gave her much pain. Tushi bathed and poulticed her legs, wrapping them in damp grass in hot weather and in soft deerskin in cold weather, but still she could not walk. She was always small, but now when Ishi carried her outside into the sunshine, he said, "A half-grown fawn is heavier in the arms than you, my mother."

Mother called Tushi "Daughter," and Tushi was reminded of Grandmother when Mother spoke in a certain way and when she laughed.

Sitting under the gray pine with her work, she followed the seasons by the changing colors in the leaves of the trees across the canyon.

Quail brought their young to the cleared space under the pine tree. The downy babies ran over Mother's feet, unafraid. Towhees came to pick up scraps of acorn bread she saved for them. She watched the owl family which, season after season, nestled on the storehouse roof.

Elder Uncle sat beside her in the sun. They talked of the Old Days while he carved out a new set of stirrers and paddles or made a pouch, and Mother sorted grasses and wove a mat, or a new hat for Tushi.

"We are the Old Ones of Wowunupo," Mother said.

Elder Uncle took a sweatbath and went to the creek to swim as often as he was able to make the steep climb back from the creek; and he went there to fish when he could, especially since he could no longer hunt deer. Ishi had made him two polished sticks of the straightest manzanita wood he could find to help him walk up and down the trail. Elder Uncle called himself "Old Four-legs" and "Badger" when he used them. He complained, "My air is getting as heavy as Grandmother's."

But he listened closely to the news Tushi and Ishi brought him of the outside world. He wanted to know where new saldu cabins were being built; whether the saldu were cutting down acorn oaks; if the deer were leaving early for the mountain; how many baskets of white acorns Ishi and Tushi expected to bring in; and when Ishi meant to go to the south side of Yuna Canyon where the best tobacco grew.

Each day Elder Uncle put offerings of tobacco just outside the village, and he made sure that Ishi regularly left some tobacco leaves at Ancestor Cave. He was the good Majapa of his People; and Mother's firepit was the brightest place in all the world; so Tushi and Ishi said to each other.

IT WAS harvest time; Tushi and Ishi were on Badger Creek where they had camped when they first came to Wowunupo. Now they were gathering acorns, which they stored in a cache under the trees to be carried home later. Tushi had spread black raspberries and manzanita berries on mats in the sun to dry; each time she passed, she stirred them with a wooden paddle so they would dry evenly.

The smoking and drying frames were hanging full of deer and salmon. As soon as the fish and meat dried and could be taken off and stored, the frames were refilled; the baskets would soon overflow.

While they picked the fat white acorns, the cousins made plans for the Harvest Feast. The harvest was large and they meant their Old Ones to have such a Feast as Ishi and Tushi remembered from Tuliyani. Mother still could not walk, but she said, "I shall walk into the New Year on my own feet. You shall see!"

Tushi was humming a song of her own; Ishi heard his bow song singing inside him. *When Tushi sings, life is good! At the Harvest Feast we will roast pine nuts and sing together. She will dance the Woman's Dance and then she will make me dance the Hunter's Dance, going west while she goes east. Mother will laugh and she will sing with Tushi while Elder Uncle beats time with his walking sticks.*

The next day, Tushi and Ishi were back on Badger Creek. Tushi gave the berries a stir, and went to the cache where Ishi was storing another basketful of acorns.

"I think I hear chopping," she said, nodding in the direction of the saldu cabin up creek from them. Ishi listened; there was the hollow thub, thub of chopping and then the crash of a felled tree.

They took cover in the brush, moving like snakes on their stomachs closer to the cabin. There they saw eight saldu with shovels, axes and saws, and the strange, tube-stick which looked to them like a firestick. They remembered it from the time the saldu changed the trail: one man looked through the tube telling another one where to lay a black rope in a straight line along the ground. Later, stakes were driven along that line every few bow-lengths.

125

Tushi did not stay; she went home to warn Elder Uncle and Mother. Ishi stayed where he could watch what the saldu did.

They do not make a trail; it is a ditch, which will take water from Badger Creek. But where is the ditch to go? . . . . Aii! The stakes point to the ledge, to Wowunupo! Do the saldu mean to make a sawmill like the one in Acorn Hollow?

At the end of the day, Ishi went home. Tushi was waiting for him at the edge of the village. They walked on past the cave and to Lookout Point where they could talk without alarming the Old Ones. They agreed the saldu would be sure to discover them if they tried to move now with Mother not able to walk; they must stay hidden in Wowunupo. Even if the ditch was dug as far as the ledge, they might be safe. The outer part of the ledge was more open, and the cave and storehouses could not be seen from there.

Said Ishi, "We can hide as the people of Three Knolls hid in their houses during the first time the saldu came."

"But we must have a plan in case they find the village."

"I can carry Mother into the brush."

"And Elder Uncle and I can go quickly down the tetna trail."

"But there is no place you could stay even for a night."

"We could cross the creek to your fishing shelter. That is hidden and it is big enough for the two of us."

And so it was decided.

The cousins sat side by side on Lookout Point, the Yahi world around and below them. That way, they said, pointing, would be Tuliyani; over there, Green Cave. They picked out the three knolls and the cliffs above Round

Meadow, their old play place. They could see the top of the Yuna waterfalls. Tushi leaned far over to see if she could see the deep pool beside Gahma.

"It is a good land," Tushi said, sitting up. "But I think I shall know how to leave it."

Ishi's lips tightened so they would not form words well. "What do you mean, Little White Shell, 'leave it?'. . . . We shall escape these saldu as we have the others, we four."

"Wanasi . . . . I think I may not escape. I have not told you, because the meaning was not clear to me, but for a moon's time now, I have dreamed the old White Dream again, night after night. It seems to me the dream is preparing me."

"Preparing you . . . . for what?"

Tushi stood up, took off her necklace with the blue and white flower beads among the shells. Twirling it in her hand so the shells sang a dry, rattle song, she said, "Look at me, Cousin-brother. I am Shell Woman! My shells sing and their song fills the air. You cannot hear the Monster, and the sound of harsh saldu voices is lost in my song. My shells sing above Tuliyani, over Wowunupo, all the way up to Waganupa.

> Wa–ku
> Hus–taya
> Shu–shu–shu!"

It was a strange song, a strange slow dance she danced to the song. *Tushi looks now as she looked the first time she danced around the fire with Grandmother's long willow wand in her hand.*

The motion of the shells slowed and stopped. Tushi put them around her neck, and sat down by Ishi. "Each night I hear the rattle of distant shells. I sing the shell song and I go a little

127

farther into the White Dream. I now smell the green grass and the many-colored flowers my mother tells me are there in the ice. Tonight I may see them as she does. One day I am sure to go to the White Land to find my mother."

Still Ishi could say nothing. "I do not wish to leave you, Tehna-Ishi. I shall not go unless I must. And . . . . when you follow me down the Trail, I shall come to your campfire." Tushi put a hand on Ishi's arm for a moment. "I shall meet you, and together we will go to the campfire of your father."

Ishi wiped his hand across his face. "Suwa! So be it, Shell Woman of Wowunupo!" Again Ishi was silent, and after a while, Tushi said, speaking softly, "Cousin, you know my Dream. Tell me yours!"

Ishi looked at his cousin. He said, "In the Old Days, Grandfather said it was only in the watgurwa a man spoke of his Dream. But . . . . these are not the Old Days, these are the Ending Days. And you, my Cousin, belong now to Shell Woman. I have wanted for many moons to tell you my Dream as you have told me yours. . . . ."

Ishi told Tushi his Dream and at the end Tushi said, "It is as I thought; there is something which you are to do."

"Do? What can I do?"

"I do not know. It is your Dream, and not to be understood by another."

They spoke no more of their dreams, but of Mother and Elder Uncle and of all they did as children, and later, together.

They stayed on Lookout Point until Sun was close to the western edge of the world. "There is the Monster, reminding you of your dream," said Tushi.

Before they left Lookout Point, Ishi took tobacco, blew a pinch in each of the Earth Directions and another over Tushi's head, making a motion with his hands as of smoke encircling her. Then they left, Tushi going to Wowunupo, Ishi down to the creek. He said he would bring salmon for the evening meal, but he went to be alone, to think over all Tushi had said, and all that had happened that day.

Su! I cannot make the sweetgrass bracelet for Tushi. She is My Cousin-sister. She is my friend, she is the Dambusa One!

> Wa–ku
> Hus–taya
> Shu–shu–shu!
>
> White Shell Beads
> Like hawk's wings
> Shu–shu–shu!

CROSSING the creek on the alder log, Ishi took his harpoon from its hiding place and swam out to a smooth flat rock almost in midstream but so sheltered under overhanging maple trees it could be seen only from the shallow sandspit on the opposite bank.

I will clean out the harpoon shelter, in case Tushi and Elder Uncle have to stay there one night.

A salmon swam past. With a quick throw, he harpooned it. He brought it to the rock and was set for another throw, his eyes looking into the water, when, from under his lids, he saw four shod feet on the sandspit. He looked up, his harpoon poised. Two saldu stood there, staring as if they saw a ghost.

Never have saldu come here! Never have they moved so quietly! I heard nothing. I smelled nothing. I was thinking only of Tushi!

"Heexai—sa! Heexai—sa!" Go away! Ishi shouted at them, waving his harpoon. They turned and ran into the brush.

Are they everywhere, those saldu? What is it they do here? Ishi waited, but no one else came and the two did not return. It was almost dark when he went home.

They made no fire in Wowunupo that night or the next morning. As soon as it was light, Ishi went part way down the creek trail. He had not gone far when he heard something coming up the trail. His bow drawn, he waited. One of the saldu of the night before came in sight crawling up the steep trail on all fours. Ishi took aim and shot, his arrow tipping the man's hat from his head. He was ready with a second arrow, but the saldu slid back down the trail and Ishi let him go; he did not mean to kill unless he must.

Hearing nothing more there, he went back to Wowunupo. The four people stayed close together at the cave entrance, Mother lying on the lip of the cave, protected by the overhanging roof. Tushi said uneasily, "Our brush-screen frightens me today. It keeps from us what we need to know."

"I'll go to the gray pine—no, don't worry," Ishi saw that Mother was about to protest. "I will go only high enough to free my ears and eyes of the brush."

He was back in a moment. "I think they may be on the ledge. I can see nothing, but I hear the sound of saldu knives, cutting through brush."

Tushi asked, "How close are they?"

"They are in the very heavy brush—I think they are close—it is hard to tell—we have never had an enemy here. . . ."

Said Elder Uncle, "They may give it up and dig the ditch another place."

Ishi did not say what both he and Elder Uncle knew—a ditch could be dug only on the ledge. He was worried. *If they are not digging, what are they doing? Setting up the guide line of stakes? Or, having seen me by the creek last night, are they searching now for a village? The one who was on the way up the trail this morning surely was not making a ditch.*

Again Ishi climbed up the gray pine. Now he heard saldu voices, grumbling, grunting sounds.

131

*There is the feel of heavy moving bodies. They
are very near! They have found one of our
tunnels, else they could not move so fast!*

A saldu face appeared at the end of the tunnel close to the storeroom shelter, from which
a little winding path led to the gray pine and
the center of the village.

Ishi jumped to the ground, just ahead of a
saldu dragging himself out of the tunnel and
standing up. He ran to the cave, calling softly
to Tushi. "Su, su! Sigaga, sigaga. Saldu! Saldu!
Run, run, you and Elder Uncle!"

There was no time to carry Mother into the
brush. Ishi threw a cape and blanket over her
and swung himself up into the nearest tree.
Looking out between the leaves, he saw Tushi,
with Elder Uncle leaning heavily on her arm,
start in the direction of the tetna trail.

They went out of sight at the instant the
saldu in the lead came to the open circle around
the gray pine where he stopped, calling out
something in a tone of surprise to those behind
him. Ishi could see little of what went on, but
he heard excited saldu voices, talking, calling,
exclaiming.

They seemed to be all over the village and
one of them found the cave. Ishi could see only
the outer edge of the cave floor, but he heard
baskets being taken from shelves inside. Then
the rabbitskin blanket, which covered Mother
and a bit of which hung out where he saw it,
moved and disappeared. A saldu must have uncovered Mother.

Below him in the cave, Mother lay still,
trembling, fearful, with Ishi poised above ready
to jump if she cried out or if anyone touched
her. But a saldu spoke to her in a quiet voice.
Ishi heard him say, "Malo?" And Mother answered, "Mahde, mahde." Sick, sick. He must

132

have been looking at her bandaged legs. He said something else, but Mother did not understand him. Others came to look, and the first one seemed to be ordering them away. There then was much talk among the saldu; Ishi thought they were quarreling. The end of it was that the one who found Mother, threw her blanket and cape on the ground and left, followed by the one who carried the tube.

Those who stayed paid no further attention to Mother, who lay helpless while they carried baskets and other articles in the cave, outside to look at in the light. Ishi caught glimpses of them fingering his tools. One of them found Tushi's unfinished basket and was showing it to the others.

Such are the saldu: they will enter even the women's house. Nothing will be in its place when these demons finish. Still, Tushi and Elder Uncle got away, and they do not touch Mother. . . . . But when will they go?

At last the voices trailed off, the last booted step went out of sound. Ishi dropped to the ground, took Mother in his arms and carried her to his work hollow. He stopped to listen and look once more, then carried her across the stretch of bare shale into the madrones and around to the far side of Lookout Point. There he put her down.

"They did not touch you? You are not in pain?"

"No pain. They did not touch me. Where are the Little One and Elder Uncle?"

"Safe. I saw them as they started down the tetna trail."

"Aiku tsub. . . . Then let those discourteous ones move on and after another sunrise or two, we will return to our firepit. . . . That one who uncovered me wished to carry me somewhere

133

I think, but the others would not have it. . . . His voice was kind."

Sun warmed the ground where Mother lay and a feathery chamise bush screened her. She said she was comfortable.

Said Ishi, "I will make sure they have not come back, and get some things from the cave."

Ishi returned to Wowunupo meaning to bring his bow and a basket of water, some food and blankets. He kept to the brush at first until he was sure no saldu had returned. No one was there. He stood under the gray pine at the center of the village, looking around. He did not find the disorder he had expected, but an emptiness, as of a long un-lived-in village.

Where is everything?

The door of the storehouse stood open, its shelves emptied. He looked behind it; there was nothing there. He went to the cave; it was empty except for Mother's treasure bundle which had been overlooked on its high shelf along with a few other things beside it. He went to the drying frames, to the smoke-house, to the watgurwa. Slowly, slowly he understood— the seeming emptiness was real.

Gone were his bow, arrows and otterskin quiver; his harpoon and firedrill; his knives, flakers and chisels; most of the kitchen and household utensils and all of the food. He looked for Tushi's raccoon and mountain lion cape, for the bearskin blanket, for Mother's feather cape, for the mended and ragged rabbitskin blankets. There was nothing.

I am dawana. I run around like Coyote, without sense. My eyes are upside down, so I do not see what is before me. I will find everything when my senses return. Meanwhile, I will say nothing to Mother of this.

Ishi searched through the brush from end to

end of the village, and in the tunnels leading from it. He found nothing.

In the cave were left one basket partly filled with water and two baskets with some berries and seeds in them. He took these and went back to Mother. She asked no questions about his bow or about blankets or food. He made her a bed of boughs and ferns. It was a warm night. He sat by Mother who, very tired, fell asleep. Wide awake, he stared into the moonlit canyon.

If I could know Tushi and Elder Uncle are safe!

The next morning, Ishi was picking some berries for Mother when he heard someone in the brush. Two saldu had returned. *Do they come for more? They will have to take the drying frames and the houses—there is nothing else.*

Ishi watched them from his hiding place in a clump of manzanita. They were the two who had left before the others the day before. Ishi felt sure now they were looking for Mother. They searched the village and surrounding brush and the length of the ledge, looking for footprints or other clues to guide them. They looked even as far as the base of Lookout Point. They sat down hot and discouraged, close to the manzanita in which Ishi was hidden. Earlier, the coat of one of them brushed the chamise bush behind which Mother lay. They did not see her; they did not hear Ishi breathe.

When they were leaving, they went again to Wowunupo. One of them stopped at the cave, and taking a pocket knife and a sack of tobacco from his pocket, put them on the lowest shelf. Then he turned away and was gone.

BLACK rainclouds hung over Waganupa as they
had for the past two days, but the weather
continued fair on Lookout Point. Mother said
firmly, when the saldu were gone, "I think those
two meant me no harm. In any case they will not
return to this place today. Go, go, my Son, to
Tushi and Elder Uncle. They may need you. I
will not move, and nothing will bother me here."

There was some water left in the basket and
there were the berries Ishi had picked. He
stood, uncertain whether to leave her.

"Go. Go to those two."

He put his hands on her shoulders for a
moment. Mother smiled at him, then he was
gone.

He did not use the tetna trail to the creek
since the saldu now knew it, but came to the
water below the trail, close to the sandspit. He
looked first across the creek where the fishing
shelter was hidden in the brush. There was
nothing to show that Tushi and Elder Uncle
were there. This was to be expected, but he was
very uneasy about them because the creek was
running high and muddy. It must have rained
heavily on the mountain during the last three
days.

Also, he had found Elder Uncle's walking
sticks in Wowunupo. Without them the alder
log would be dangerous for him to cross. Nor
was there any place for two people to have
stayed on the Wowunupo side: the canyon wall

and the creek bank were too steep, and today, much of the creek bank was flooded. Water covered the sandspit itself and the tracks of the saldu of two nights before were under water. Ishi started upstream to the alder log, keeping his eyes on the wet ground, on the chance of finding more footprints. And so it was he saw something bright lying in the mud where the swirling waters threw spray and small pebbles and sand from the creek.

He knelt to see what it was: a bit of deerskin cord, and strung on the cord, two white shell beads and a broken fragment of a white and blue bead. *Tushi's necklace! The piece from Green Cave! The white shells I bored and strung for her myself!*

Forgetting the saldu, forgetting Mother, Ishi ran up the bank to the wet alder log and across it to the fishing shelter. It was as he had last seen it. Tushi and Elder Uncle were not there.

He ran back across the creek where he had found the beads, and looked up and down the creek bank. Then he went to the tetna trail. On the trail he found faint footprints, and marks as if Tushi and Elder Uncle had slid down the last, steepest part. Ishi thought it was not that Elder Uncle had fallen, but that sliding was the only way for him to get down without his walking sticks.

Ishi searched above and below the alder log and in the brush along the bank. There was no mark of a foot, or of a hand; no strand of hair caught on a thorny bush. The brush was as empty as Wowunupo. The message of the beads was clear. The spray still washed, high and frightening, over the slippery log.

He jumped into the water, grabbing a branch from the flood. Using it to brace himself against the force of the high water, he started to search the creek. The branch was swept away, and he lost his footing. The flood knocked him against boulders in midstream, forced him into a whirlpool and spun him round and round. He was carried downstream and thrown onto the bank far below the sandspit.

He lay, breathing hard, half-unconscious, while his strength slowly returned. When he could he went again into the creek, walking or swimming, back to the alder log. It seemed not possible to fight the flood, but he had its measure now, and he knew the creekbed as he knew the dry trails. Trying not to give way to panic, bracing against the boulders, diving to the bottom of the deepest parts, he satisfied himself he had covered the pockets and the roughest places and the shallow pools, from the alder log to where the canyon began to open out.

Could they be below the canyon, where the creek widens, where the saldu houses begin? As far as the River Daha? Was it this my Dream was telling me?

He threw himself back into the water. *I shall go to the Daha! I shall follow them!*

He turned to the bank and pulled himself heavily from the water. *Su, su, Sun was high when I left Mother! She is alone all this time, not able to move! Now Sun is far to the west!*

Ishi stopped to take an old basket from the fishing shelter. He recrossed the creek to the Wowunupo side, filled the basket with water, and climbed steadily up to Lookout Point. He was bruised in his body and in his heart. Mother greeted him quietly, asking no questions.

She had not been idle. She had picked whatever she could reach, dug up some shoots of old, tough greens and a few late bulbs, and she had shaken the ripe seeds from the grasses nearby. She gave the handful of seeds to Ishi, saying,

"Eat them, all of them. I have been tasting all day."

Ishi told her what she knew from his face as soon as she saw him—that he had not found Elder Uncle and Tushi. To each other they said, those two would come to Lookout Point before many days; they had found another place to stay because of the flood. Ishi said nothing to Mother about the beads.

Again the night was warm and Mother slept or pretended to sleep. Ishi sat looking into the darkness of the canyon, into the darkness in his mind. The next day he went to Badger Creek. No saldu were to be seen, but their axes and shovels were leaned against the fence.

Again he went to Banya Creek. He searched the creek and both banks from Gahma above the adler log to the end of the canyon below it. He went to the places near the creek where he and Tushi had gone together many, many times; places where Tushi would know he would look for her. He left the creek and went to the top of the ridge and along the ridge. Tushi and Elder Uncle were not in any of these places, nor was there any trace of them.

ISHI kept no count of the days or the nights or of the changing moon. He must have slept, he did not remember where or when. Somehow, he carried Mother down the steep canyon side and across the alder log to the little fishing shelter. Here was water, and nets, fish lines and hooks and a few odds and bits of baskets and mats, an old scraper or two, and a broken obsidian knife —all that was left with which to begin again.

There was food as long as the weather held: ripe berries and nuts and fish. Banya Creek was no longer flooding; Ishi caught small salmon and trout in a net or with hook and line, or by playing his hands in the water in fishlike motions. Fish swam into them as though the hands were shadows of other fish.

He made a firedrill from a rough slab of cedar which he found by the creek, gouging a single socket and groove in it. For a drill he used a stick of poison oak. The socket and drill were not a very good fit; it took him a long and weary time to get a spark. At last the tiny bit of frayed milkweed rope which lay in the groove as tinder, caught fire, and from it, a handful of dry grass. Ishi blew softly on the new fire, adding chips of wood until it was a sure blaze. Mother nursed this New Fire when Ishi was away or asleep; it was not allowed to become cold until Ishi had made a drill, hardened and straightened with the help of the fire itself.

There were no cooking baskets. They cooked in the water basket until Ishi could get some resin to waterproof a larger basket. He caught more fish than they ate; he set up a frame and hung the extra fish in strips to dry. The pieces were more torn apart than cut, for he had to use the broken, dull knife.

He brought some of the acorns from the un-plundered store on Badger Creek where he and Tushi were working when she first heard the saldu; and ground the acorns between rocks which he used as they came from the creek, without shaping them. Mother cooked the coarse and unevenly ground meal slowly, making it into a mush they could eat.

He set out snares and nets and kept the feathers and skins of even the smallest birds and four-footers he caught. Mother fitted these together. She had no needle, but Ishi punched lines of matching holes in them with a sharp piece of antler bone, and she laced them together with milkweed string. First it was a neck ruff; it grew to cover her shoulders; and before the snow moons came it was a cape, the top feathers, the lower part fox and squirrel.

These and many other things Ishi did. Mother still could not walk, but she did what she could, never complaining. She and Ishi talked about the fishing, about the four-footers which were making winter nests and burrows by the creek, about the late flights of ducks and geese. They used the old phrases in speaking; and when they finished a meal, Ishi said to Mother as Elder Uncle used to, "The acorn mush is fresh and sweet at your firepit, my Mother." And Mother answered, "There is a Son who hunts for me, a wanasi, a good hunter."

The baskets from which they ate were clumsy new-grass ones or such old, frayed baskets as they found at the shelter. Mother served the mush with a stick which Ishi had shaped roughly with the help of the broken knife and fire.

All this time, Ishi did not know at the end of a day what he had done. He moved as one whose soul has gone wandering in the night and does not return with the daylight. His father's Spirit or Jupka must have directed his hands and mind.

Mother watches me closely each time I leave, each time I return. She thinks only of those others, and wishes to talk of them. I, too, wish to talk to her. But I cannot speak of them; I cannot bear to have her speak of them. Ishi went to the fire and burned off his hair a little closer to his head; and mixing charcoal with pitch, freshened the mourning stripes painted across his face. Still Mother said nothing, and she tried to hide from him her tears.

Each day, Ishi crossed the alder log and went downstream to the place where he had found the beads. There he took them from the moleskin bundle in which he kept them, and holding them close in his hand, said a prayer and blew tobacco upward, downward, to the east, the north, the west, and the south. Then it seemed to him he heard Tushi's voice, faint but familiar, repeating their brush call, flika flika! And Elder Uncle's deeper call, gagka gagka!

He went in the direction of these calls, looking for footprints, for a bush from which berries had been stripped. He searched the woods, the brush, behind every boulder, in every cave up and down the canyon and outside the canyon. If he saw a buzzard overhead, he found the carrion it was circling above. He smelled out a mountain lion's kill, a bear's, even a fox's.

The last of the harvest moons gave way to a rain moon which grew full and then old. The first of the winter moons brought a light fall of snow. Ishi stayed home instead of crossing the creek as usual. He piled earth against the little shelter to protect it from snow and wind. Mother sat close to the fire while he did this, weaving a mat. When she spoke it was to ask, "Are you not crossing the creek today, my Son? It will be dark soon."

Ishi shook his head. "It is no good. I cannot find them."

Mother spoke very low. "They are not here, Wanasi, else you would have found them long since." Ishi came to Mother. Her arms around him, they cried together, and those were good tears which broke the moon-long, held-in, lonely grief. And in this way, they again spoke of Elder Uncle and Tushi, although they never used their names, but called them the Lost Ones.

Said Mother, "It may be hard for those Lost Ones to put their feet on the Trail, but the Old One has much wisdom and the Little One dreamed a White Shell Dream. They will find the Trail one day."

There was a deep fall of snow. Mother looked at the white world. "It will be easier for those Lost Ones, now there is no more smell of flowers to draw them back to the brush." Each night Mother poured out the water from the water basket. She and Ishi well knew that flowers or a basket of water will tempt a Spirit to linger, to smell and to taste, and so lose its way again.

It was a winter of heavy snow. But the snow lay as a rabbitskin blanket on the land. Sun shone bright and there was not much wind; Ishi kept the fire going day and night. Mother was warm and dry in the little earth-covered shelter.

One day they were talking by the fire while Ishi skinned a rabbit. Mother said, "You again look like a hunter."

"Su!" He held up the rabbit. "A rabbit wanasi, eh?"

"Never mind—deer or rabbit—you are like your father. Very like him. . . . Suwa! I no longer fear for you, my Son."

Ishi smiled at Mother when she said these

143

words. There was much tenderness in her eyes, in the soft voice.

It was morning, five risings of Sun later. Ishi got up early to throw fresh logs on the fire. It was not full daylight, but the fire reflecting against a snowbank lighted Mother's face. She was asleep, the heavy lids closed, the lips curved in a Yahi-bow half smile. She was curled up like a child, one hand cradled against her cheek. On the slim wrist Ishi saw the worn old sweet-grass bracelet which she usually kept in her treasure bundle.

It was Mother's final sleep. She had taken leave of the beloved son, Tehna-Ishi, to go to his father.

ISHI carried Mother to Ancestor Cave. There he made for her the cleansing funeral fire, after which he buried her with her few treasures, her digging stick, and a basket of acorn meal. She was with her Ancestors, with the Old Ones and the Restless One, with the One whose sweetgrass bracelet she wore.

When all this was done and the stone slab back in its place in the cave, Ishi returned to the fishing shelter. All strength and purpose left him and there followed a time of no memory, of nothingness. He remembered nothing afterward of the rest of the winter. It was not until the warm days of the New Year that his soul returned to his body and he was able to rouse himself to make a fire and take a sweat-bath.

He plunged into Banya Creek just before two saldu came along the bank of the creek. Letting his head go under water, he swam quietly downstream until he was away from them.

Thus I swam in my Dream; thus I could swim on, coming at last to Outer Ocean. Old Salmon could tell me if the Lost Ones came also to Outer Ocean.

Ishi swam on and on; the creek began to widen, its flow less swift; he was almost out of the canyon. Then he was sure he heard the Little One calling him, from a great distance, from far up the canyon, toward the mountain Waganupa. He turned back and swam upstream. The saldu were gone. Tiredly, he pulled himself from the water and went to the fishing shelter.

Ahh! While my soul has wandered, those Lost Ones have been calling me! I shall go to Waganupa and find there a house of flint. Soon I must use flint dust for a cape, for I have no other; and the smoke of the sacred tobacco will have to do me for food.

He took with him the broken knife, a sort of child's bow he had made while Mother was in the shelter with him, some fish nets and snares, two old baskets, his firedrill, pouch and treasure bundle, and went slowly with many stops to rest, to Upper Meadow. There, he went back and forth across the meadow many times, thinking he heard the voices of the Lost Ones, always in another part from where he was.

Living in this way, a sickness entered his body. He could not eat and he was very weak. It seemed to him he heard the Old Lost One saying to him, "Remember, Porcupine is a friend to all Yahi. Only if a Yahi is starving and has lost his bow and arrows and his harpoon and is too weak to hunt and fish may he kill and eat Porcupine. This is the rule because he is so easy to kill." Then Ishi killed and ate porcupine. The sickness left his body; his mind cleared; he could walk and trap and fish again.

He left the meadow and went to the mountain, looking for a house of flint in which to live. On the slope of Waganupa he found a cave which was dark, but warm and dry.

It seems to me this is the cave the Restless One was looking for. Grandfather once said,

"Waganupa is different from other mountains, being warm inside. This is because when the People were first made, two Heroes went inside the mountain to live." Those two may not mind if I come to live near them for a little while.

He made new fire inside the cave and turned to go out for rocks to block the entrance, but a brown bear was already coming in. He yelled at her, and without looking or thinking what he did, grabbed a blazing branch from the fire. The bear reared on her hind feet and swiped at him, tearing the flesh of his arm and shoulder. At the same time, he shoved the burning branch into her open mouth. She bit down on it; then, with a roar of pain and fright, backed away.

Somehow, when she was gone, Ishi gathered a few mountain herbs by the stream below the cave and poulticed and tied up his arm and shoulder. He even rolled rocks in front of the cave entrance. He lost much blood from the wound the bear gave him, which added to his weakness. Of the coming of the snows he had no memory. Shut up in his house of flint, there followed for Ishi another time of no memory, of nothingness.

He was asleep; then, suddenly he was awake and on his feet. Outside he heard plainly the Little One calling flika flika, and he heard the Old Lost One calling gagka gagka! They were close, the voices strong, not faint, not far away.

Hurriedly, Ishi rolled one of the rocks aside and plunged, naked, into the icy night. The world was white, as it was with Mother in the fishing shelter. The boughs of the pines were heavy with snow, and icicles hung from them. The night was brilliant and the Five Sisters danced overhead.

Ishi answered the calls. Hearing nothing

more, he ran higher and higher up the mountain, calling, calling, crying, praying. He ran till dawn but he heard only the wind moaning over the ice fields and saw only the Dancing Sisters in the midwinter sky.

At dawn he returned to the cave. Across its mouth hung a line of sharp-pointed, glistening icicles. *It is the Little One's White Dream! The Lost Ones are safe! That is what they tried to tell me.*

Stiff with cold and weariness, sobbing from the shock of the brief closeness of the Spirits of the two Lost Ones, he stumbled in the snow but recovered and crawled under the protecting line of icicles so as not to disturb them: they were sacred to him—the icicles of White Shell Woman.

Inside the cave, he rolled the rock in place and fell, unconscious, onto the bough bed at the back of the cave.

ROUGH WINDS of spring blew off the mountain; warm rains melted the snow which poured in floods into the meadows and creeks. The radiance of Sun's plumed headdress filled the sky and warmed the earth.

Ishi peered from the mouth of the cave on the steep slope of Waganupa. As he tried to chew a piece of stale jerky, there came to him,

148

carried on a warm breeze from the foothills below, the sweet smell of new clover.

He pushed aside one of the rocks which blocked the entrance to the cave, and crawled outside. The brightness blinded him. He sat down, shielding his eyes with his hand. *Su, su! The old world is renewing itself once again!*

His eyes became used to the brightness, and Sun warmed him. He rubbed his elbows and knees, bending them, unbending them. *Bay leaves and hot water and a good sweating are what you need! You are as stiff as old tetna at the end of his winter sleep. . . . How many moons have you been in this darkness?* Ishi rubbed his hand across his eyes.

A brown bear with a young cub came from a clump of pine trees below the cave, passing close to Ishi but paying no attention to him. Seeing her, Ishi's shoulder ached with the old pain; he thought he saw a scar on the lips of this bear.

Su! Are you the one who tried to tear off my arm? We are friends now? It was not always so. You too wanted a house of flint. Why, I wonder, did I not let you have this one? What do I do here? And what is this jerky I am chewing?

Ishi got up and went into the cave, looking about inside as if he had never seen it until this morning.

This is not deer jerky—what do I eat? And what do I do with this squirrel's bow? He tossed the bow to one side and picked up the broken knife. There were husks of acorns and empty pine cones on the floor. He swept them outside. There was no food in the cave.

He lay down on the bough bed. *Su! This is where I sleep? Why? . . . . Why did I not sleep as my Mother slept, without waking? . . . . It was the voices of the Lost Ones which*

149

held me to life. But I do not hear those voices now. As he lay looking up at the cave ceiling, a memory of the night of midwinter and the White Dream came back to him. He sat up; he tried to stand up, forgetting the cave was too low.

No wonder I walk like tetna! There shall be no more of this sleeping in darkness, this half-standing like a four-footer on his hind legs! Ishi rolled the rocks away from the cave entrance and strewed stones and earth over the fireplace. *Mother Bear can see the cave is empty, she and her cub. New Fire shall not again be made in this place.*

He went to the creek where he washed and drank the sweet melted snow water of Waganupa. Downcreek from him, Mother Bear nudged her cub out of the water and started it back uphill. *Go in peace, tetna. We have understood each other well enough.*

Ishi knew he must eat soon; he was light-headed from hunger, and his joints ached as he walked painfully down the steep mountainside. *I must find a little strength, enough to take me once through the Yahi World. I must make sure the Lost Ones' Spirits no longer cry out to me, no longer need me.*

He spent the first night away from the cave at the edge of Upper Meadow. There he ate new clover and sweet young bulbs. His sleep was dreamless and he wakened less stiff and lame. He recalled when he was there a few moons back—how the Lost Ones seemed to him to be everywhere except where he could reach them. Now the meadow was without any Spirit presence. The yellow of the marsh marigolds was like a second sun; Ishi surprised himself laughing as he and the Little One used to laugh, walking on marigolds, their bare feet sunk deep in the cool black sludge of the boggy meadow.

The marigolds made him think of Round Meadow. *I will go to Yuna Canyon, to the places the Little One and I went when we were children. If I have not understood the White Dream, it is there I might find some trace of the Lost Ones.*

Ishi went to Three Knolls, to Black Rock, Tuliyani, Round Meadow, even to the beaver dam. The beavers were at work; the young of deer and rabbit, of quail and fox, played in the meadow.

When we left this canyon, the brother of my father prayed that the marks of the People should go under the earth and that the feet of the saldu should catch in the high brush. . . . And now I see these things are coming to pass; the marks of the People are almost gone; the World is becoming as it was in the beginning; and the saldu here are uneasy, they live as strangers. Soon the canyon will have forgotten them.

The spring days grew longer and warmer. The heat moons were over the earth and summer came early, hot and dry. The strength Ishi had drawn from the renewing days of green clover and new salmon faded even as the greens of the grasses turned to yellow and burned ochre under the heat of Sun's plumed headdress in a cloudless sky.

Always moving, restless, on guard lest a saldu surprise him, Ishi had been to all the old places in Yuna Canyon by midsummer. He went, panting, hungry and weak, to the pines above Three Knolls where it was a little cooler. There he lived as he could until the heat moons were on the wane.

151

Then he crossed over the ridge to Banya Canyon, taking the old familiar way down the canyon to Ancestor Cave, where he burned tobacco and pine resin, praying while the fragrant smoke filled the cave.

No Spirit Presence remains here. I am the last of the People; when I am gone, it will be as though they had never been.

He left Ancestor Cave and went down into the canyon to the alder tree crossing. He found the fishing shelter weatherworn but untouched. There he made a fire, took a sweatbath, and slipped into Banya Creek. The water felt good, but the swimming left him breathless, gasping. He was barely able to pull himself up on the flat rock where he had been fishing the evening the two saldu appeared on the sandspit.

He lay face down, hands hanging limp in the water. When he opened his eyes he saw his

reflection in the still pool. *My eyes are like Elder Uncle's as they were the last moons of his life, sunk deep in their sockets and inward looking, not the eyes of a hunter.*

He saw a face thinner and more lined than

152

Elder Uncle's, with hair dull and bristly, for he kept his hair burned off close to his head in mourning for Mother and the Lost Ones.

He rested until he was stronger, then swam back upstream to Gahma. The crescent of land, the dark, reflecting water, were as on the day Jupka gave the world to the Yahi People. But the houses were fallen in, four-footers had dug and rooted there, and saldu had littered Gahma with broken bottles and tin cans.

Ishi walked again under the overhanging branches downstream to the creekbank where he had found the Little One's necklace beads. As he expected, this place, too, was empty of sound and meaning, and he turned away from Banya Creek. Slowly he climbed up the steep canyon wall, stopping to get his breath under the pine tree where he had shot off the saldu's hat. Going on again, pulling himself from bush to bush on all fours, he reached the level ledge and was in Wowunupo.

The drying frames were blown over, the storehouse roof was gone, the reservoir filled with leaves, its sides crumbled. Poison oak was beginning to grow into the clearing around the gray pine. No four-footers had rooted there —none larger than mice and squirrels and chipmunks. Nor had any saldu been there.

A few more moons of wind and rain, and what we made here will be gone. There will be again the empty cave, Wowunupo-mu-tetna, Grizzly Bear's Hiding Place.

Ishi felt something sharp against his foot. He reached down and picked up the broken fragment of an arrowhead. *This I made from a white hard material the Restless One and I found on the mountain.* He let the broken head drop back onto the floor of the cave where he found also a bit of one of his mother's basket-

153

hats. His heart hurt him when he saw it. He slipped it inside his belt.

Lying on the lowest shelf of the cave and red with rust was the small pocket knife the saldu had put there, and beside it, the rotting sack of saldu tobacco. As at an earlier time, Ishi did not touch them. He was tired, but he walked slowly on, climbing up to Lookout Point. It was not the time of day for the Monster nor was he thinking of the Monster. The only sounds were a dove's low, moaning call from somewhere in the canyon, and the summer rustle of leaves. Picking a cluster of bay leaves, he crushed them in his hands and took deep breaths of their cool, pungent smell.

A little kaltsuna lizard joined him on top of Lookout Point, pumping itself up and down on short front legs, the chest puffed out. Ishi stroked the lizard with one forefinger and it became quiet. He laughed. "So," he said, "you are here, Little Brother. You will be here always, I think."

Ishi lay on his back gazing into the arching Sky World. A jupka butterfly settled for a moment on his hand. He watched the slow fanning of the delicate wings. "You, too, are here, O Great One?" He raised his hand till he could look into the strange butterfly eyes. "The People you made are no more, O Jupka. Only the land remains, and you, and Kaltsuna, here beside me. Perhaps you know all this? Perhaps it is as well if you do not know."

Ishi lay in the hot sun, his eyes closed. *The White Dream spoke truly. It is finished, the long search for the Lost Ones. They found the Trail through the ice and are in the Land of the Dead. There is nothing to wait for in this empty land, nothing—I am free to go. I will go to the Little One and the other Lost One; to the Restless One;*

154

to the firepit of my Ancestors. And there I will find my mother and my father.

Ishi left Lookout Point and returned to the Wowunupo ledge where his workplace used to be. He turned down canyon, to the west. The trail beyond the ledge was dim, but he knew this trail joined another, broader, plainer trail a little farther down—the Trail to the Land of the Dead.

It is not far. Each step brings me closer. Suwa! Aiku tsub!

4

TO THE EDGE OF THE WORLD

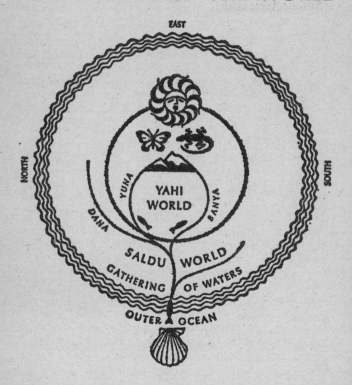

DARKNESS overtook Ishi; nights of no moon. He could no longer see where he stepped, where he stood. He had expected to be on the broad Trail long before now.

It is no matter. The journey is begun. I will find the trail soon; it cannot be much farther.

Weak from hunger and tired in his bones and in his heart, he lay down and slept. His was an uneasy sleep. In his dreams he continued his journey which took him into a wild, strange land. Loose rocks rolled under his feet, tripping him. Worst of all, winged demons pecked at his face and pulled at his arms and tried to push him off the trail. At first dawn, their screeching woke him.

He looked around, one quick look before the demons were on him again. There was no sign of the trail he was looking for; the hills, dark against the rising sun, were not the hills he knew. He lay on the ground, crumpled against a corral fence; the bitter stench of slaughtering filled his nostrils, and he smelled saldu and saldu dogs.

Hanging over the fence were cattle hides and on the other side of the corral was a saldu slaughterhouse. Yapping, whining and threatening him was a ring of dogs. Beyond the dogs were five or six saldu, also threatening him with their firesticks. Ishi did not move.

Why do those demons not explode their firesticks? I am without even the hunting bow of my father.

But the saldu beat the dogs off. Careful not to come too close to Ishi, they kept their firesticks pointed at him.

For what do they wait? They wish to hang me? Let them! Let them take my scalp. . . . Su, su! They show fear. What can they fear from the last Yahi? He has no knife, no bow;

*he is already half-dead. It will soon be over,
their fear and mine.*

Ishi closed his eyes, opening them only when
some time had passed and a wagon drove up
bringing more saldu. One of the newcomers
was a Headman; the others addressed him as
"Sheriff." The sheriff walked directly to Ishi,
spoke to him in a quiet voice, helped him up
from the ground, and without roughness,
fastened his wrists together with rings of a hard
material. He then brought an apron which had
been worn by someone while butchering—it was
dirty and bloodstained—and put it around Ishi's
shoulders.

The sheriff nodded toward the wagon. Between fright and weakness and the smell of
stale blood and saldu sweat, Ishi was light-
headed. He stumbled, but the sheriff steadied
him, holding his arm, and helped him to the
high wagon seat beside him. The wagon lurched
as the horses started, and Ishi almost fell off.
The sheriff stopped the horses long enough to
free his wrists so that he could hold on. The
others, in the seat behind, grumbled when he
did this, but he spoke sharply to them, and they
said no more.

Ishi had seen wagons drawn by horses, but
this was the first time he was ever in a wagon.
Down the road ahead, he saw a large oak
tree, and beyond the tree, houses at the edge of
a saldu village. The sheriff slowed the horses
to a walk.

*We come now to the hanging tree, the oak
which is an acorn oak.*

But the sheriff did not stop under the tree;
he continued into the village and down its main
street. He went slowly because people came out
of the houses and gathered around the wagon,
talking and staring. The sheriff had to order

them away from the wheels in order to keep
moving.

*My uncle has told me this is how the saldu
behave at a hanging. They press close, women,
children, the Old Ones, everyone, as at a Feast
or a Round Dance.*

They stopped in front of a large house, the
sheriff's house. The sheriff motioned Ishi to
come with him into the house. Inside, he took
him to a small room without windows and
separated from a larger room by bars.

The outer room filled almost at once with the
crowd which had followed the wagon. Men
leaned on the bars staring at Ishi and saying
words to him which he could not understand.
When he answered, "Nize ah Yahi"—I am of
the People, a Yahi—they laughed. The sheriff's
helper brought a tray on which was a cup of
coffee, a bowl of soup and bread. He offered it to
Ishi, who shook his head.

*The food and drink are probably poisoned.
In any case, I do not eat while these saldu of
no manners, these noisy demons, stare at me.*

Ishi moved as far away from the bars as he
could. He sat on the stone floor, leaned his
head against the wall, and closed his eyes and
his mind from the saldu who stared at him. He
tried to recall the nights before.

*What Mechi-Kuwi, Demon Doctor, guided my
feet to this land? Did I walk while I slept?
Where am I now? How shall my Spirit, when
they finish with me here, find its way back to
the Trail?*

Through the wall there came to Ishi's ears
a faint familiar breathy call, Whu–HOOH–huu!
The call was repeated, plainer, nearer. With a
noise as of falling rocks, the Monster passed
just outside the Sheriff's house.

The house shook and settled; the Monster

slowed and stopped. Ishi could hear its deep, panting breath. After some moments, its breathing became heavier and it moved away, going out of sound.

Ishi shook himself. He was surprised to see that the house stood, that all was as it had been. *Su, su. I am within the Dream! Was it Kaltsuna and Jupka who led me, sleeping, off the Trail? Do they mean me to cross the Great Valley to the River Daha and to follow it to Outer Ocean?*

More saldu crowded into the room, put their faces against the bars and tried to make Ishi talk. They laughed and spat tobacco juice. The air was thick and foul. After some hours the sheriff came with more food, but Ishi shook his head.

Will he say I must eat? It is no matter; I cannot.

Someone laughed when Ishi turned away from the offered food. The sheriff said some words; he did not raise his voice, but the room became quiet. He pointed toward the outside. At first no one moved; he spoke again; the crowd began to move draggingly toward the entrance. There were a few underbreath comments. This time when the sheriff spoke, his hand moved toward the firestick in his belt. There was a rush as of stampeding deer, then the room was empty except for the sheriff, his helper, and Ishi.

The sheriff turned to Ishi and said something of which Ishi understood the meaning if not the words. "This is better?"

His eyes were kind when he spoke. Ishi answered, "Aiku tsub!" And he recollected his uncle's words, spoken long ago in the watgurwa in Tuliyani, "Not all saldu are bad. Remember this in the moons to come when I am no longer with you."

160

The sheriff gave Ishi a cigar, and taking a fresh one for himself, lighted the two cigars with a quick-fire stick. When Ishi had taken a few puffs on his cigar, the sheriff smiled, and, slowly, Ishi returned the smile.

The helper went out, coming back with a clean saldu shirt and pants. He motioned to Ishi to put them on. Ishi made signs to him that he wished to wash, and the helper placed a bucket of water and a towel in the room, at the same time taking away the dirty apron Ishi had been wearing. Ishi washed as well as he could.

This is like Grandfather and Grandmother with their one basket of water in Wowunupo.

When he was clean and had rid himself of the worst of the smell of the slaughterhouse, he put on the clumsy saldu clothes. *This stuff is such as the walls and tops of wagons are made of. Su—it is in any case clean. And the Headman seems pleased that I wear it.*

Once again, the sheriff offered Ishi something to eat. *This man has not the eyes of a poisoner. He is kind and it is a rudeness to refuse.*

Ishi ate a few mouthfuls of the strange food and drank some water. Again the sheriff smiled and said some pleasant words. Ishi, too, smiled. "Aiku tsub!"

The sheriff let a few people come in. They tried to talk to Ishi and he tried to answer, but they could not understand each other. *They know nothing of the tongue of the People. It is no matter except the Headman is disappointed.*

Then the Monster returned. *Never has there been such a noise! It is as when Waganupa shakes and boulders roll into the canyons. It is also as the coming of a noisy friend. I wish I might see the Earth-Shaker! This watgurwa has not even a smokehole.*

161

Before leaving for the night, the sheriff brought a cup of coffee which Ishi drank. Then he pointed to the frame of pine wood with wagon cloth stretched across it, which stood in one corner of the room. Ishi lay down on the strange bed.

He was tired, tired. He listened to the saldu sounds in the dark: the tramp of booted feet; loud laughter; the explosion of a firestick. The saldu sounds grew fewer and died away; there were only familiar night sounds: a mouse gnawing in the wall; crickets singing in a tree and the distant screech of an owl.

So ended Ishi's first day in the Saldu World. When the sheriff looked in to say goodnight, Ishi's eyes were closed and he did not open them. He was slipping into sleep; he did not wish to rouse himself.

Perhaps my Dream will lead me back to the lost Trail.

BUT HIS Dream did not lead Ishi to the Trail. He wakened the next morning in the room with the bars and it was the voice of the Monster which wakened him.

162

Later in the morning, a stranger came to the sheriff's house. Ishi observed him closely; he was different from any saldu he had seen.

The Headman appears pleased to see him. They grab each other's right hands. It is thus the saldu greet each other. This one comes from a distance—he carries a travel bundle. His clothes are not clumsy; they follow the line of the body. He wears the hair on the face, but it appears to be trimmed with a sharp knife or other tool. He does not spit tobacco juice. . . . His eyes are different, without the coyote look of those who stare through the bars. He carries no knife or firestick in his belt. He and the Headman speak together; they speak of me. Now the Headman brings him to me. Su! I shall do the handgrabbing since it is expected.

No! He sees I do not wish to handgrab. He sits beside me. His smile is good; he does not have the strong saldu smell. He reaches into his pouch and brings out pieces of white bark with blue markings on them like little birds' footmarks in the dust. . . . Now he looks closely at the markings, and he says something to me. . . .

What should I answer?

He looks again at the bird tracks and says something else. The sounds remind me of the songs which Grandfather learned from people who lived on the far side of Waganupa before the saldu came. Now he speaks as the Lost One once told me the People to the north of Yuna Creek spoke.

Aii! What does the saldu say? Siwini?

Ishi spoke for the first time since the Stranger came into the room. He repeated the word, siwini, and patted the frame of the bed.

The Stranger nodded, yes. "Siwini, pine."

163

The Stranger said, "Auna, fire."

Ishi repeated, "Auna," and made the motion of lighting a quick-fire stick.

The Stranger laughed and nodded, yes, again. Ishi studied the pieces of white bark. *I make nothing of the saldu magic, but it is powerful. These bird tracks cause the Stranger to speak in the Tongue of the People. Perhaps it is a trick? Perhaps I am dawana and dream I hear the Tongue again after the many moons of silence? I shall try speaking to him.*

Said Ishi, "Moocha?"

The Stranger looked down his line of bird tracks, then he repeated, "Moocha," and, taking out a pouch, opened it. "Moocha?—tobacco?" Ishi nodded.

Said the Stranger, "Hildaga."

Ishi pointed to the Sky World, spreading his fingers to mean many hildaga, many stars.

Said Ishi, "Wakara?"

The Stranger pointed upwards and cupped his hands. "Wakara, moon."

Then he said, "Daana." Ishi held his arms as if cradling a baby, a daana.

Ishi said, Wowi." The Stranger pointed around the small room. "Wowi, home."

Ishi shrugged, and they both smiled when he said, "Wowi." *Is this place of no smokehole my home?. . . . Ayii! It is no matter; the Stranger and I say words to each other.*

After a while the single words grew to short questions and answers. *We speak the Tongue! Even my Dream did not reveal such magic! My strength returns as I speak again! There are many unsaid words which have choked me since the morning the Lost Ones went out of sight down the tetna trail; since my mother slept off during the white night.*

Now the unsaid words poured out faster than

164

the Stranger could mark them down or find them in his lists: words of loneliness, of searching, of hunger, of cave-living alone. *The Stranger listens. Sometimes he knows the words; sometimes he understands by signs and by what my voice tells him beyond the words. And because he understands, I cannot stop speaking. . . . But now after much speaking, I am very tired.*

Ishi lay down on the bed, unable to say anything more. The Stranger left him for a while, making him understand he would be back when Sun was straight overhead in the Sky World.

Ishi half-slept, half-dreamed; the word siwini, siwini, siwini weaving through his dream.

The Stranger came back as he said he would. They spoke together now slowly, quietly. By the end of the day they had traded many words; they were beginning to speak as friends who talk together.

I no longer think of firesticks and the hanging tree and food into which poison has been put. I wait to speak the Tongue, to hear this Stranger speak it.

Ishi's sleep was dreamless that night. He wakened to the first faraway Whu! of the Monster. That morning the mush and the muddy drink, coffee, tasted good to him.

With the Stranger's help, the sheriff talked to Ishi. He asked him if he wished to return to the Yahi World. And he said he would help him find it if he wanted to go there. Ishi shook his head.

To the Stranger he said, "The kind saldu Headman does not know that World is no more."

Then, asked the sheriff, would he like to go to a Reservation? Some of the People who used to live in the Valley would be there.

Again Ishi shook his head. To the Stranger he said, "He speaks of the Fat Ones of short memory and full stomachs, the Forgetters of the Way."

Said the Stranger, "Come to my house with me. It is a museum-watgurwa. I think you will like it there."

"Is it far away?"

"Haxa, yes. It is where the River Daha and other rivers empty into Outer Ocean."

Aii-ya! This is the Dream. Surely the Stranger does not speak of the Edge of the World? "One reaches the museum-watgurwa by wagon?"

"No, by train." The stranger imitated the breathy Whu-HOOH-huu of the Monster.

"The—train—draws a wagon?"

Ishi sounded so unbelieving, the Stranger asked, "You have seen the train?"

"Many times. But from far away, from Lookout Point and from Black Rock. Even from Waganupa. I have known it since I walked the trails alone. . . . It enters my dreams; it is my friend."

"I wish also to enter your dreams; to be your friend. Will you come with me in the train?"

Ishi touched the Stranger's shoulder lightly. "You speak the Tongue of the People; you are my friend, Majapa, museum-Majapa. I will go with you to your watgurwa."

The next day, Ishi was up before daylight. The sheriff helped him dress: underwear, shirt, tie, stockings, shoes. Ishi looked down at himself when he was dressed. "Tck. Tck. A saldu-Yahi!" He walked up and down the room several times. Then he sat down and took off the shoes and stockings and handed them back to the sheriff.

Majapa came just then, and Ishi said to him,

"Now I know—nothing is wrong with saldu feet. It is what you call shoes that are wrong." He looked at Majapa's shoes. "How do you know where you walk when your feet do not touch the earth?"

"We mostly do not know where we walk."

"I think I am turning into a saldu. The night I came here my feet did not know where they walked."

Majapa laughed. "Do not fear, you will not turn into a saldu. But I thank your feet for bringing you where I could find you. . . . You know, I looked for you before; but to tell you of this I must first learn to speak more words of Yahi."

This is a strange one, this new Friend. What does he mean? He is like the Power Dream, not to be known or understood at once.

Ishi, the sheriff and Majapa walked to the railway station. And there, beside the station, the Monster stood panting. It was bigger, blacker, more powerful than Ishi had imagined anything could be. After a moment of hesitation, he moved closer to it, drawn by his old and friendly feeling for it. He measured his own height against the great black wheels. He looked at its smoking head. To Majapa he said, "Truly it is the Smoky One. The smoke pours as from a God's pipe. The head and face are those of an Earth-Shaker. Jupka and Kaltsuna were right to turn my feet toward this wonder."

The sheriff shook hands with Ishi and said, "Good luck!" Ishi said, "Good luck!" and followed Majapa into the train. Almost as soon as they were seated, the Monster began to pull the train, slowly, then faster and faster into the Dream, deeper and deeper into the World of the Saldu.

The plik, plikety plik of wheels rolling over

rails fitted an old Yahi song which Ishi used to sing with his bow:

> Yahina—weh,
> Yahina—ini,
> Yahina—weh,
> Yahina—ini.

He sang it soundlessly to himself now; it helped him to look past the passengers who stared at his burned-off hair, at his bare feet.

Ishi looked out the window. On all sides spread the great valley, of which he had seen narrow glimpses from Black Rock and Lookout Point. He drew in his breath with wonder.

The Great Valley is broader than the largest meadow. Not one, but many rivers flow in bends and curves across it. The acorn oaks grow tall and heavy with acorns here. And the ripening grasses cover the earth! Once the Valley People and the valley deer grew fat here and there were many of them. Now the saldu and their cattle fatten here. Many saldu! They are everywhere. . . . too many saldu!

Yahina—weh, Yahina—ini! The telegraph poles streamed by in time to the song, in time to the wheels' plikety plik! The pictures in the window changed so fast that horses and houses and telegraph poles and people blurred and melted into one another.

Sun had almost finished his day's trip over the sky when the Monster came to the gathering of waters where two rivers, the Daha the larger of them, flowed together, and became one. Ishi smelled the distant salty smell of Outer Ocean. He and Majapa and the other passengers left the Monster, and rode on something Majapa called a ferryboat.

The ferryboat floats on the waters of the

rivers as the newly fished-up World must once have floated on Outer Ocean.

"This is Outer Ocean?" Ishi asked Majapa.

"This is the bay." Majapa pointed west across the water to two headlands. "Beyond the headlands is Outer Ocean."

"It is larger than I remember. In my Dream I was swimming and there was much I did not see."

Ishi and Majapa leaned over the railing to look at the water rolling, wave after wave beneath and beyond the boat. Sun left the edge of the earth, plunging into the ocean. Said Ishi, "This water is not like the water of Banya Creek."

"No, this water is salty."

Ishi nodded. "The salt of Outer Ocean is different also from the salt of our meadows."

There came the shrill, thin call of seagulls; the lost moan of foghorns. Sun's plumes disappeared beneath the waves; the waves turned green-black as they rolled on and on between the headlands and were swallowed up in Outer Ocean.

The rock-glass, green-black waves of Waganupa! The mountain which was the center of the World, the canyons and creeks of home floated before Ishi's eyes, awakening a homesickness which made him dizzy. *The rock-glass waves go on forever, too big, too many. . . . Su, su! To be safe in Ancestor Cave, where there is no sound, no brightness—a dead world.*

Stiff with weariness, Ishi followed Majapa off the ferryboat, and into a trolley car which took them far, far into the City. The trolley car jolted and jerked; it fitted no song Ishi knew. The City was a strange shining place of stars fallen from the Sky World, lighting up endless broad trails as far as the eye could see.

Then they were off the trolley car, and

169

Majapa was holding Ishi's arm, guiding him up a long flight of stone steps. Before them was a heavy door. Majapa found his keys and unlocked the door of a house of stone.

"This is Flint Man's House?"

"This is the museum-watgurwa."

Majapa led the way through many rooms and upstairs, switching on a light as they entered a room and switching it off as they left it. At last Majapa put down the bag he was carrying.

"This is your room." He opened the curtains, turned back the covers of the bed. "Here is the clothes closet; here the bathroom."

He helped Ishi to undress, to get into the large bed. He pulled the blankets up over him. "You will be all right?"

"All right."

"Look, here is the switch. To make your room dark, push the dark button. To bring the light, push the white button. Shall I turn the light out for you?"

"Out."

"I will come for you in the morning. Sleep well—good night."

"Good night."

WHEN Ishi wakened, Sun was shining full in his face. He thought he was on Lookout Point, but then he saw he was in a room and lying in a bed. *The room with the bars! But there are no bars, and the blanket which covers me is soft like Mother's feather cape.*

Ishi got out of bed and went to the window. Below him was a long flight of stone steps leading to a green bank. Beyond were a steep street with houses facing onto it, a forest of which he saw only the green tops of the trees, and bare, abrupt hills and blue water.

Blurred memories came back to him: of the Monster, a trolley car, a ferryboat, seagulls, foghorns. *The City—this is the City, the museum-watgurwa. But where is my friend?*

He saw his clothes lying across a chair. Slowly he dressed. It was not easy to do. By the time he finished buttoning the shirt collar and knotting the tie he could no longer look at the window view.

The world is too big here. In this watgurwa I am as far from the ground as at the top of the gray pine in Wowunupo. If I leave this room, I will be more lost than when I missed the Trail. He swallowed hard, feeling only his lostness

171

and strangeness. *Why did Jupka not keep my feet on the Trail?*

There was a knock at the door; it was Majapa. *He makes no sign that he smells my fear.*

His friend asked if he had slept well; if he was hungry. "It is breakfast time," he said.

They went down a long hall and downstairs to the museum dining room where several museum men were already gathered around the table. They shook hands with Ishi and repeated the words, "Welcome, welcome to the museum."

Ishi answered, "Welcome, welcome!" And one of the men patted his shoulder and said, "Good, very good!"

For breakfast, there was oatmeal mush. They asked Ishi if it was as good as acorn mush. He nodded politely. "Haxa—it is good with a little salt. The milk of the cow spoils it." There was also the muddy saldu drink, coffee; and bread, bacon and eggs.

Do they have to go far to find the nests with the eggs? Perhaps it would not be a polite question.

The museum men did not stare at his hair or his bare feet. They knew a few words of Yahi and they listened closely when he spoke. "It is as in the Old Days when my grandfather sat at the firepit of neighbors; friendly and courteous people speaking a different tongue," said Ishi to Majapa.

The museum men do not press in upon me; their voices are quiet.

After breakfast, Majapa took Ishi to his office, and then to a room where there were many bows and arrows. He opened the cases in which the bows were kept and motioned Ishi to take them out if he wished. One by one, Ishi examined each bow. Some were made of juniper or other wood he knew; some of wood which

172

was strange to him. He felt their grip, their weight, and he held them in position to string and bend. Some of the bows were of great age; Ishi knew they would break if they were to be strung and bent. Majapa explained that they had lain in caves or been buried in the ground for many moons.

I could make arrows fly from these bows. But the Peoples who made them are not known to me: Algonquin, Comanche, Navajo, says Majapa; and Persian, Scythian, Macedonian; the names sing as the singing of my lost bow. Aii-ya! To shoot, to shoot the bow again! To see arrows flying from these warrior bows!

"You have no Yahi bow here."

"I have never seen one."

"They are different from these. I could make a Yahi bow for you, but I have no tools."

"We shall see. Perhaps we can find the tools."

We talk more words today than yesterday. My friend's Yahi words are sometimes not right. But he listens when I speak. And always he makes more of the bird tracks on the white bark which he keeps in his pocket. Then he says the words over to me, many times until he says them in the true Yahi way. It is as when I make a fine arrowpoint, using smaller and finer flaking tools, the way Katsuna would do it.

Ishi repeated over and over the saldu names: train, trolley car, ferryboat. He listened to the talk of the museum men and soon knew the names of the different foods which came to the museum dining table. He learned the saldu names of the furniture in his room: bed and chair and table and lamp. And he learned the name of each person he met, repeated it and remembered it. He was beginning to speak the saldu tongue.

A Kuwi, a Doctor, came to the bow room

with his young son to meet Ishi. They were friends of Majapa. Ishi smiled at the boy, saying to his father, "This is a fine wanasi. Is he to be a hunter, or will he have power over certain pains?"

The Doctor shook his head. "Who knows?" he said. "He is a dreamer, this one."

"Aiku tsub. And what do you wish to do?" Ishi turned to the boy.

Majapa translated and when he understood, the boy smiled and said, "I wish to be a hunter. Will you teach me to make and shoot a bow?"

"Haxa, haxa!—yes, yes! You and I will be wanasi; we will hunt for this museum-wat-gurwa."

Majapa asked if the Kuwi might examine Ishi to be sure he had no pains, no Mechi-Kuwi, Demon Doctor, sickness. Ishi nodded, "Haxa."

Will this saldu Kuwi have the skill of the Old One of Tuliyani?

He soon saw the Kuwi was wise in the ways of doctoring. He felt the pulse and listened to the breath go in and out, and pressed the places which are tender if a pain has somehow entered the body.

The Kuwi said Ishi had no pains. He asked him how the Yahi treated snakebite and stomach cramps. Ishi told him and in turn asked the Kuwi if he had the power to extract pains.

"Some power," said the Kuwi. "As you see . . . ." He took a strong medicine the size of a pine nut which he kept in a capsule in his black pouch. He placed it in Ishi's right ear, and a moment later, pulled it from Ishi's left arm-pit. He then laid it on his own hand. It was gone. He motioned to Ishi to reach into his pocket and there the medicine was!

Said Ishi, "I believe you have very good control over your medicine."

They went outside where Majapa smoked his pipe and Ishi and the Kuwi smoked cigarettes. The smoke was light and sweet, like sacred tobacco; it drifted away toward Outer Ocean while they talked a little of hunting with the bow. They went down the high museum steps, past the rows of white houses, to the forest Ishi had seen from his window and which the saldu called a park. It was quiet there, with trails leading into the brush, and ponds with ducks and geese and swans, and an open hillside with buffalo and antelope.

So passed Ishi's first day in the museum-watgurwa. After dinner, in the evening, Majapa came to Ishi's room. Ishi's few clothes, his treasure bundle, and whatever other articles he owned were neatly put away on shelves. A pot of tea was on the table and Ishi and one of the museum men were sitting, drinking tea.

Majapa motioned around the room. "You like? Aizuna—It is your own."

Ishi smiled. "Wowi aizuna, wowi aizuna." My own home.

He waved goodnight to Majapa and turned back to his visitor who was telling him about fishing in Outer Ocean. That much of the story was clear to Ishi. For the rest, he understood only a word here and there, but he knew fishing stories, and he was sure this was a good one. *When I know more saldu talk I will tell this museum man a fishing story.*

Said Ishi to Majapa the next day, "This watgurwa is bigger than the whole village of Wowunupo."

"Will you take me to visit Wowunupo in the time of the spring salmon?"

Ishi shook his head. "It is a dead world."

"I think it is not dead. You remember it, and I remember it."

Does this Friend own a Power Dream which takes him upstream with the salmon? How else could he remember the Yahi World? Sometime I think he may tell me his Dream.

THE NEXT day, Majapa took Ishi to a room where there were baskets, nothing but baskets. Said Majapa, "These baskets do not come from across the ocean as do some of the bows. They are all from Peoples like the Yahi who lived on the land before the coming of the saldu."

Ishi nodded, then turned to the baskets, looking at them shelf by shelf, row by row, until he came to a certain row where he stopped.

"These are the baskets of my People." He spoke then almost in a whisper, "But how is it the Museum-watgurwa has these baskets?" He pointed to two, side by side.

Majapa looked at the two baskets. "They are Yahi, are they not?"

"These baskets were made by my Cousin. She made them in Wowunupo." Ishi sat down on a bench. There was a weakness in his legs; his heart pressed against his chest; slow tears formed in his eyes.

These are the Little One's baskets—but this kind saldu, my Friend, was not among those who came to Wowunupo. I saw their faces; I heard their voices; his was not one of them. How do these baskets come here?

Majapa had put the two baskets beside him on the bench; Ishi did not touch them. "My Friend, you speak sometimes as if you were once in the Yahi World, I know not whether on a Dream journey or a waking one. It was not you who found these baskets?"

"No, no! I saw no baskets in the Yahi World. . . . You remember the saldu who came to Wowunupo?"

"Haxa."

"There was one who spoke to your mother?"

"Haxa. I remember that one."

"He did not steal from Wowunupo?"

"He took nothing. He spoke with courtesy to my mother."

"And he returned the next day and tried to find your mother?"

"Haxa."

"This one came to the City, to the museum-watgurwa to tell me about finding your village and about the Old One there who had a sickness in her legs. As soon as I could—it was not until the end of the heat moons, a long time—I went to the Great Valley, and he and I made our way into Wowunupo. For the length of a moon we searched for you . . . for your mother. We found nobody, nothing. . . ."

"Why did you wish to find her?"

"We knew she could not be alone, and that whoever was with her was without tools or blankets. . . . We hoped we could help. . . . We were too late. . . ."

Ishi's thoughts went back to two saldu he had swum away from, after Mother was gone, and of other saldu he had seen from time to time. *Majapa was not one of them. He must have come to Wowunupo while I was looking for the Lost Ones in Upper Meadow.*

But Majapa was speaking. "Someone in the sheriff's village sent these baskets to the museum, two moons ago. I put them with other baskets most like them. . . . Here. . . . They are yours. . . ."

Majapa picked up one and started to remove the museum label, but Ishi stopped him, waving his hand, palm out, back and forth. "Let the museum mark stay. My cousin's baskets are part of this watgurwa of treasures." He took the basket which Majapa held out to him, and picked up the second one, bringing them to his face, smelling them. "Aahh! The smell of the cave, of Wowunupo, is in them!" He traced with a finger the design woven into one of them. "This is a fern stem. It came from Round Meadow. This is iris. The Little One and I found it across the creek, high up. . . . Su! The Little One becomes part of the Saldu World, even as I."

Later in the day, Ishi came to Majapa with a question. "About the two saldu who did not steal from Wowunupo—you know them—why did they not stop the others from stealing?"

"I asked that question. They tried to stop them, but the Headman would do nothing. . . . There are good and bad Headmen among us, as there are good and bad people under the Headmen."

"So said my uncle to me long ago."

"The two we speak of did not work for that Headman after the day they tried to find your mother. It is with us as with you—the one who does not agree with the Majapa must leave the watgurwa."

It was the next day. Majapa said, "It is time we go to Outer Ocean."

Again they rode on a trolley car, but this one took them away from the City and around a high bluff which reminded Ishi of Lookout Point. The bluff was one of the headlands which Majapa called the Golden Gate, where the rivers empty into Outer Ocean. And there, below them, and as far westward as the eye could see and farther yet, was Outer Ocean.

Close to shore were black rocks where sea lions slept, and climbed and slithered off into the water. Their barking and the crying of seagulls could be heard over the roar of the waves. Ishi and Majapa walked down a slope which brought them to the wet and sandy shore, to the Edge of the World.

A wind off the water blew their hair on end and sent salt spray into their mouths and eyes. They laughed and ran toward the waves, and when the waves were about to pour over them, they ran back up the wet sand away from them. One wave brought a perfect white shell to the shore; Ishi stooped to pick it up, and he thought of his Dream.

Majapa and Ishi sat on a driftwood log and smoked. They did not try to talk over the ocean noise. *Majapa is perhaps in his Dream as I am in mine.*

Before they left, Majapa took some cornmeal from a little leather pouch. He blew a pinch of it onto the nearest wave, which carried it out to sea.

"I learned to make this offering from one like you, who lives far inland, but who also keeps shells from Outer Ocean in his treasure bundle, and who sometimes leaves his desert home to visit the ocean."

"It is a good gift. From this day, I will make a gift of acorn meal to Outer Ocean if that seems good to you?"

"Aiku tsub. It seems good, very good to me."

They walked away from the sea on sand which had been washed so far inland it was dry and hot to the feet. Ishi's feet sank deep into the sand; he caught his breath. A feeling as of quick fire rose through his feet and legs into his belly and chest, to his head; he closed his eyes.

I walk with the Little One on the hot stones of the canyon floor; we are on our way to Round Meadow to play the Meadow Game.

He opened his eyes. *Su! It is with Majapa I walk, through the sands of the Edge of the World. Outer Ocean brings to me a shell like the shells of the Little One's necklace. Her baskets are in my room in the museum-wat-gurwa. Thus and thus our Dreams, the Little One's and mine, come close.*

They walked inland to the park and across the park, stopping to look at the buffalo. Ishi asked, "Is it true, what the Kuwi's son, Maliwal, says, that Peoples like the Yahi once shot the buffalo with bow and arrow, as we shot the deer?"

Majapa nodded. "Those people ate the buffalo meat and used the bone and hides as you used the meat and hide and bones of the deer."

Ishi gazed at the buffalo. "When Maliwal learns to shoot the bow, you and he and I will come here and hunt the buffalo, h'm?"

They went for some distance farther, until Ishi stopped, pointing up hill. "Wowi, wowi aizuna!" He was looking and pointing at the museum-watgurwa high above them.

When they had climbed the hill and the high, stone steps, they turned to look down at the park and to pick out as many landmarks of their walk as they could see. Ishi swept his arm across the view. "We walked all around your World today."

"It is also your World now."

"Haxa, yes. Your World and mine."

A WHOLE moon came and went and another was on the wane. Ishi sat at the top of the museum steps, looking down to the trees in the park below and out to the headlands of the Golden Gate, and his thoughts scattered as they used to do when he sat on Black Rock.

He thought of the Trail which he missed and he thought of Wowunupo. Wowunupo, empty, plundered. Wowunupo with hot fire in the firepit, and the Old Ones and the Lost Ones sitting around the fire. He heard again the murmur of their voices. But then his thoughts came back to Majapa and the museum men; to the museum-watgurwa; to the cigarette he was rolling as Majapa had showed him.

He went from room to room in the museum. He was beginning to know this watgurwa as he knew the storehouses and the cave at Wo-wunupo. He studied the feather headdresses, the deerskin leggings, the house of buffalo hides, the carved wooden boxes, the masks, the totem poles, the baskets and all the other treasures to be found there. These things were new to him, but he knew what tools had fashioned them; he knew how the hand had held the tool.

There were rooms where broken pottery and glass and bone objects were mended; where furs and hides were cleaned; where treasures were made ready to show to the men and women and children who filled the museum in the afternoons to look at them. In one of these workrooms he found a piece of rock-glass, straight-grained and without a flaw, which had been thrown aside. There were also some flaking tools, not the best, but good enough. Ishi made a pad of wagon cloth to protect his hand from the glass and set to work. Later in the morning he walked into the office and laid an arrowhead on Majapa's desk.

"This is very fine workmanship," Majapa said, looking at it through a magnifying glass. "Where did you find it?"

"I made it."

"Where? How?"

"Come. I show you."

They went to the workroom. Ishi showed Majapa the horn flaker he had used to make the arrowhead. "But to make an arrowhead worthy of Kaltsuna, I use a finer flaker. . . . I could make such a flaker. . . . I could make arrowheads . . . . a harpoon . . . a bow such as Maliwal wants. . . . The good tools which were on the shelves in Wowunupo. . . . They could sit on the shelves of the museum-watgurwa. . . . If you like?"

"I like very, very much. You will make a Yahi room here in the museum. Visitors will see a Yahi bow and a Yahi harpoon. In your room they will learn something of the Yahi World."

Some of the materials Ishi needed were already in the museum. Many kinds of wood, and ferns and grasses and dyes he found in the park, or in country close to the City. He and Maliwal took long trolley car rides to out-of-the-way places, coming home with good juniper or rock-glass. And as often as the museum men went into the country, they brought back something Ishi had said he needed. The shelves in his room began to look like the shelves in Wowunupo.

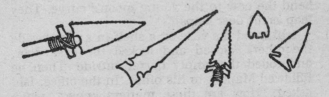

One day Ishi looked up from his work; he heard an express wagon drive up. This usually meant more treasure from some distant place; he hurried to open the basement door and help bring in a large barrel. He pried off the top of the barrel, and by the time Majapa came, Ishi was well along with the unpacking.

The new treasure was pottery, pale earth-colors, painted in red earth-colors and outlined in black. Ishi sucked in his breath with wonder. "These are the colors of our baskets. One could keep water and cook and carry in these as in baskets?" One by one he handed them to Majapa as he unpacked them.

"Yes, they were once so used. They are old, very old."

"From what World do they come, Majapa?"

"From the Greek World—a place in some ways like the Yahi World."

"The Yahi World has no baskets of clay."

"No—I meant the Greek World was flat like the Yahi World and was surrounded by an Outer Ocean which was known as the River Ocean. . . . There were Gods and Heroes, and in the center of the Greek World was a mountain, which was called Olympus."

Ishi held one of the ancient Greek vases at arm's length, studying the pictures painted on it. "Aii-ya! Here is one who shoots the bow!" He looked at another. "Here they hunt! They hunt a deer! The Greek wanasi are strong; they bend the bow to the young moon's curve. They leap as the deer leaps!"

Ishi stood the vase on a shelf in a case beside the others, closed and locked the case door, and rolled the empty barrel outside. Then he followed Majapa to his office. In the office, Ishi asked, "How are these matters known, when as you say, the Greek World was a world of long ago?"

Majapa took a book from the bookcase behind his desk and opening it to a certain page on which there was a drawing, showed it to Ishi. "It says here, 'The Ancient Greek World.' You see the World, and the River Ocean all around it. The words on this page and other pages tell the stories of the Greek Gods and Heroes."

"You can make a picture such as this one?"

On a pad of yellow paper, Majapa drew an outline of hills, a mountain and streams. Pointing to the mountain, he said, "Here is Waganupa." And pointing to the streams, "Here is Yuna Creek; here, Banya; here the River Daha." He wrote in the names. "Where is Wowunupo?"

Ishi studied the picture. "Here." He made a dot. Majapa wrote the name underneath.

"Here is Gahma," said Ishi. Then he drew a line of dots. "This is the trail from Tuliyani to Three Knolls." He made a small circle for Black Rock and a larger one for Green Cave. Again Majapa wrote the names, and then read, pointing to them, "Daha, Wowunupo, Gahma."

Ishi made a drawing on another piece of yellow paper, with lines for boundaries and half-circles for villages and dots for trails. Majapa wrote the names as he said them. It was a picture-map of the Yahi World. When it was finished, Ishi asked, "You could tell the story of the Old Ones? You could make a book?"

"Yes. It could begin with your map-picture. It could have the Yahi words you have told me, and as many more as you wished to say." He motioned to the row of notebooks on his desk. "Many moons after you and I have traveled the Trail of the Dead, those living in distant worlds could read and know how the People spoke and who were their Gods and Heroes and what was their Way . . . . if you like."

"I like. Aiku tsub. I will speak the Tongue; you will write much Yahi. The Old Ones will live in a book."

THE MOONS completed the circle of the seasons once, twice, and twice again. Ishi sat outside the museum at the top of the stone steps, knotting a fish net of milkweed fiber, looking up from his work to watch the brightly painted fishing boats returning from Outer Ocean with an early morning catch.

The Kuwi stopped for a moment to see what he was making and to look at the fishing boats. "I think they bring fresh salmon today," Ishi said to him.

People passed on the embankment below. Most of them called a "Good Morning" to Ishi who waved and aswered their greeting.

Majapa came out and sat down beside him. "This is the fourth return of the day when you first came to the museum-watgurwa," he said.

"Su, su! That day seems as far away as the days in Tuliyani."

"I should like to see Tuliyani, and Yuna Canyon."

"You still wish this?"

"Yes. Your Dream brought you to the Edge of the World. But I was born at the edge of the world and my dream carries me up the rivers

186

to the creeks to the hills. . . . I went inland once where I made friends with some Old Ones who taught me what they remembered of the Tongue of their Grandfathers. This tongue was enough like your own that you and I could speak together when we met, you remember?"

Ishi smiled. "I remember well, Majapa."

"I made the waking trip when I looked for you in Banya Canyon, and went to Wowunupo; but only in my dream have I been to the top of Waganupa and to the bottom of the gorge of Yuna Canyon."

"You are young, Majapa. The Dream takes its own time."

"Su, it is good to dream." Majapa took out a sack and paper from his pocket and rolled two cigarettes, giving one to Ishi. Ishi put aside his work to strike a match. He lit the cigarettes and watched the match burn out.

"This quick-fire at the end of the little stick is the best saldu magic."

"Sometimes it seems to me it is coyote magic —bad."

Ishi looked at Majapa to see if he was making a joke: he was not. Said Ishi, "I speak as one who has known what it is to find the firepit cold, and to be without any firedrill . . . . but you, Majapa, are perhaps thinking that firesticks are also quick-fire?"

"Haxa, yes. Firesticks, and all the rest; cannons, machine guns, war." There followed a silence between them.

Then Ishi asked, "The war which goes on now, Across-the-other-Ocean-War, it will come to this world?"

"Perhaps not, not this time. But we will go across the ocean to fight in this war. Or so I believe."

"You would go, Majapa?"

"Haxa."

"But you are a man of peace. You shoot at the target and hit the bull's eye, shooting better than the Kuwi's son or I. Yet you will not go with us to shoot even a rabbit for our dinner."

"Yes, I am a man of peace. But there will be no choice."

"Tell me, Majapa, for what reasons do these Peoples make a war between them?"

Majapa told Ishi something of the events which led to the World War. Ishi listened closely and at the end, he nodded. "The country, Belgium, is like the Yahi World when the saldu came among the People," said Ishi. "But the People of Belgium will not all be killed as were the Yahi, since some of the neighbors fight with them."

"Even so, it may not be enough. The enemy is powerful."

"Then you will fight this enemy?"

"Haxa. . . . But now we must work, eh?"

They went inside, Majapa to his office, Ishi to his work corner where he spread a wagon-cloth to catch the glass which flaked off in the making of an arrowhead, and the shavings from making arrows or a bow. Yahi bows and arrows, fishing nets and many tools now sat on the shelf next to the Little One's baskets.

"The shelves fill as do your notebooks," Ishi sometimes said when Majapa came to sit on the wagon-cloth with him, watching what he did, and describing it as well as he could in the notebook. They interrupted their work often while Ishi repeated the Yahi words for whatever he was doing, and Majapa said them back to him until they were both satisfied.

But today his work did not hold him long. People—visitors to the museum—came by and stopped. Usually he liked to talk to them, to ask

188

them, if they were interested and friendly, to sit for awhile with him. But the talk of war had made these strange saldu appear to Ishi as enemies; his enemies and Majapa's. He shook out his wagon-cloth, folded it, and went outside. He did not often leave the museum alone; he had had enough of being alone. But today he went to Outer Ocean by himself.

There, the wind drove the fog over sand and water in a cold white stream. The foghorns moaned like the loon bird in the meadows. Ishi stood alone on the wet sand at the Edge of the World, facing the wind and fog, thinking of Majapa, of the war, while the cold waves ran round his bare feet and left their gift of a white shell.

Ishi picked up the shell, putting it in his treasure bundle. He took a handful of acorn meal, scattering it in a wide arc over the waves at his feet. As he watched it spread, quiet on the water, he said a prayer:

Suwa!
It is the Old Evil once again!
Violence and Death and Fear and Hatred!

May the enemy who would destroy the Way
Be himself destroyed.
May he go under the earth and be carried away
Into the Ocean of Black Pitch!

May the acorn meal
Spreading—spreading—
Give its strength
To the Followers of the Way

Quieting men's hearts
As it quiets the waves
In Outer Ocean. Suwa!

189

His own heart quieted, Ishi turned away from the ocean, and went home to the museum. Now, the wagon-cloth was once again a good place to sit and work. And the people who came to speak with him were no longer enemies; they were good people, people who smiled when they spoke, who sat with him on the wagon-cloth, learning what it was he did, telling him something of what they thought and did.

SEVERAL times a week, while Ishi was at work, or when he left the museum, the Kuwi's son would be with him. Ishi it was who gave him the name, Maliwal, Young Wolf. To Young Wolf, Ishi was Elder Brother. Together they made a bow and arrows and a quiver. Maliwal learned to shoot his bow in the park where Ishi set up targets, some on the ground, others at shoulder height, and some high. He set them for close shooting and for longer distances.

Maliwal became skilled with the bow; he learned to call game to him; he moved silently through brush and over rough ground, barefoot. When he could do all these things, and knew the spoor of the different brush dwellers and could begin to tell, from the smell of the ground, what he would find there and what sort of four-footers had recently trod it, then they went beyond the park. Sometimes they took blankets and stayed out overnight. Supper for them would be surf fish if they were beside the sea, or freshwater fish if they were by a freshwater stream, or a squirrel or rabbit stew or a broiled quail if they were inland.

Maliwal and Ishi did not regard these times together as play or fun, happy as they were, and much as they liked what they did. Maliwal was much too serious about learning whatever Elder Brother would teach him; and as for Ishi, there was meaning beyond what they did.

This slim wanasi looks to me, the Old One, the Wise One, as I once looked to Elder Uncle. And, when he shoots his bow, the arrow goes beyond the target, from this World of the Monster, to the Ancient Yahi World. The arc of the arrow brings the two Worlds close.

Sometimes, when Maliwal had been with him, and then said goodbye for that time, a terrible homesickness came over Ishi. He ached to hear Tushi's soft brush voice, because Maliwal had brought it briefly nearer; he needed to feel that she moved noiselessly in the brush behind him; and if he turned, she would be there, smiling at him.

At such times, Ishi left the museum by the back door, and, taking a few steps away from the building, was lost to sight in Sutro Forest. The forest began at the bottom of the steep hill behind the museum, covered the hill, continued on the far side, westward, and on over lower hills, almost to Outer Ocean where the trees thinned, and sand dunes, bare and treeless, took their place.

The trees of the forest were eucalyptus, old, gray-green, closer to the Sky World than the tallest pine tree. Ishi knew no trees like them. He lay on the ground watching the wind blow their flint-colored leaves into wild circle dances, and breathing in the air which came from them, heavy with an herby perfume like bay and juniper together.

No City sounds disturbed the dry rattle voice of the blowing leaves. A deep arroyo cut through the forest, and at the bottom of the arroyo there flowed a small stream fed by a spring. Rabbits, skunks, mice, snakes, quail, towhees and woodpeckers lived in the arroyo, and there were occasional coyotes and foxes, but no deer.

Ishi was sure, having tried to chew the bitter, oil-filled leaves, that deer would not care for them.

The City, the saldu, have forgotten this place. The four-footers and birds here see me as a brush creature like themselves. They do not run from me; they have never heard a firestick. This is a good place and I think it has known no other two-footer.

One sunny morning his homesickness for Tushi had sent him to the forest. He sat for a while beside a green pond in the arroyo. Tadpoles lived in the pond and frogs and water snakes. Pond lilies grew there and birds came to bathe in the green water.

Ishi left the pond and went slowly up the arroyo. It became steeper and the water plashed softly over rocks. There was no other sound. A little farther on, five-finger ferns and low sedge-grass grew where the spring came out of the hillside.

One could stand on those flat rocks and drink from the spring without wetting the feet. This is the sort of place the Little Lost One liked. She said, "Where the water comes fresh from the earth, it is sweet with the taste of bulbs and fern roots." I can see her there now, a foot on each stone, bending over, drinking.

The small girl who bent over drinking from the arroyo spring was not Ishi's Little One. When she straightened up from her long drink, he saw she was a saldu child with blond hair and blue eyes. But her bare feet, and her arms and face and neck were sunburned as dark as Ishi's. She was the size of the Little One when she was first allowed to go to Round Meadow with Ishi, and this one, too, was slim and quick-moving.

When she turned away from the spring and saw Ishi, he smiled at her. She too smiled, accepting him as did the other brush creatures. Ishi held his hand up, palm out, fingers spread; she understood this signal of silence. He pointed to a fern. She looked where he pointed, and as unmoving as Ishi, stood still while a green snake glided from under the fern, over her bare feet, and into the water.

She and Ishi followed the course of the green snake downstream until it reached the pond which it crossed, disappearing in the grass on the other side. Below the pond, the little girl had started a dam. She showed it to Ishi and together they worked on it. Ishi split a flat rock which was too large for the dam, and showed her how beavers slap mud into the cracks between rocks and sticks.

Sun was almost at the top of the sky; it was

lunchtime. They walked down the trail by the creek together; then Ishi went in the direction of the museum and the little girl the other way, to her home. For as long as they could see each other, they turned back to wave.

Ishi and the little girl saw each other many times after their first meeting, always in the forest. She was the only saldu he ever knew who never asked his name or where he lived.

She believes I live in the forest, as I believe she must live there.

She came to the museum one day, several moons after Ishi first found her by the spring. He saw her and smiled at her but he did not try to talk to her in the museum.

I think she is with her father and mother. They do not talk with me, so she does not. She is shy like a fawn when she sees me in this watgurwa, but she is not startled when she comes on me in the forest. Suwa! We are two-footers of the brush, she and I. Our place to talk is in the arroyo, not here with many saldu.

This Little One was quieter even than Tushi had been. She did not ask many questions, and usually she waited for Ishi to speak. She might say, "There is a family of skunks—come—I will show you." She sat as long and as unmoving as he when they were waiting for a rabbit to come out of the brush. Quail ran into her cupped hands as fearlessly as into Ishi's.

Once they walked to the far end of the forest and back. When they were together it was Ishi who decided how far they should go; he who led the way. She followed after him as the other Little One used to follow him; and, like her, she sometimes chattered on, but in a soft voice; and if he wished to say anything, she was quiet and listened.

One day, she took a branch of young eucalyptus, the leaves curved, light green, and trailed them in the water where Sun shone on them.

"I want you to see," she said to Ishi. "They are so pretty."

She says pretty as the Little Lost One said dambusa. She calls flowers pretty, and the blue needleflies which shoot over the green pond here, as they used to shoot over Round Meadow.

They gathered eucalyptus seedpods, the largest, fattest ones they could find, and Ishi strung their beadlike caps on a cord, making a necklace for her.

When this Litte One says in her brush-voice, "They are pretty, pretty," then that other Little Lost One seems very near to me. Dambusa. Dambusa.

THE EXPRESSMAN came to the museum with a bundle for Ishi. "Please sign here," he said.

Ishi signed on the blank line of the yellow slip: Ishi. Then he went with the unopened bundle to Majapa's office. He supposed it was cedar bark or feathers or wood for arrows. *Whatever it is, there is magic in treasure bundles from faraway places. They are like the shells of Outer Ocean which came into the hands of the People after passing through many hands on their way up the River Daha and the creeks to the Yuna and Banya villages.*

Ishi measured the slender bundle. *It is the length of my arm to the tips of my fingers. . . .*

My name looks strange in square letters, not the way Majapa showed me to make them. . . . What can be in this bundle? . . . . Su! These knots are hard to untie, but it is good string, not to be made of no-use by cutting. And this is good paper.

Ishi wound the string into a little ball and folded the outside wrapping, then the inside wrappings. The treasure lay open on the table.

"Aaaah! Su!" Ishi touched the otterskin quiver with his fingertips. "My own quiver from Wowunupo!" There was a smaller bundle inside the quiver. He opened it; it was his old rock-glass knife in its squirrelskin case. A piece of paper with writing on it was with the knife. Ishi's eyes and mind blurred; he turned to Majapa. "By what magic do these come here to me?"

Majapa shook his head. Ishi handed him the paper with the writing. "What does it say?"

Majapa read aloud, " 'Dear Mister Ishi, For a long time I have had an unquiet heart that you are without your quiver and your knife. And so I send them to you at the museum where I am told you now live. I took good care of them after they were given to me.' It is signed, 'A friend.' "

Majapa was called away; he handed the paper back to Ishi who folded it and put it into his pocket; then sat, holding his treasure, touching it.

This quiver and knife do not come to me by chance. Did Jupka or Kaltsuna put it in the mind of the saldu to send them? . . . . And why should this package make me think of Majapa's dream? . . . . He has said nothing of the dream since we talked of the war.

It was much later when Majapa returned. Ishi spoke with some effort. "I have waited to speak with you. . . . We, you and Maliwal and I, could go to the Yahi World at the time of the New Year. . . . If you like. . . . I could show you the places on the map pictures. . . . We could take this knife and this quiver and the new bows and arrows which I have made in the museum-watgurwa."

THE ROLLS and bundles for the trip were packed, waiting, in the museum-watgurwa. The cold, end-of-winter moon grew old, and the new, green-clover moon hung like a bent Yahi bow in the evening sky, then grew full and round.

"It is time to go," said Ishi. *Thus begins the Dream. But today we follow Majapa's Dream, away from the Edge of the World. Whether this is good or not good I cannot now know. It is right to live the Dream, but the Old Ones may be angered that I bring with me saldu, even that I return to the empty land. . . .*

The Monster brought Ishi, Majapa and Maliwal up the Great Valley as far as a saldu village at the edge of the hills where Banya Creek flowed from the end of the canyon into the valley. There they loaded onto pack horses the bows, harpoon, baskets, bundles and blankets which they had brought from the museum-watgurwa. They rode horseback into the hills, and followed a trail above Banya Canyon. It was midafternoon when they came to Badger Creek, close to the old saldu cabin and to the oak trees where Ishi and the Little One had been gathering acorns the morning the saldu began work on the ditch.

New clover, a soft mat, covered the hillsides and rough boulders of the Yahi World. Buttercups and poppies, lupines and mariposa lilies, irises and trilliums were in bloom in the meadows and in the canyons; the air was sweet with the smell of madrone and azaleas and manzanita in white bloom. And Ishi came home.

Ishi was too uneasy, too unsure of what awaited them in the Yahi World to think much about the horseback ride, but he knew he did not like it. He was relieved when he was off the horse and on his own feet; when the packs were off the horses, and packer and horses gone.

Majapa asked, "Shall we make a first camp here?"

"We could. . . ." Ishi's voice trailed off in uncertainty.

"You are thinking of another place?"

"We could make a cache of the things we do not need tonight. . . ." Ishi did not say he had in mind the cache where he and the Little One had stored acorns. "Then we could go to Banya Creek—to Gahma." *If we stay here where saldu have made their camps over many moons, will the Spirits of the Ancestors know that these saldu, my Friends, are different from those others?*

"Then let us do that," said Majapa.

"It is a rough trip between here and Gahma."

"But when we are in Gahma, we are where your life began. . . ."

Ishi nodded. *My Friend is truly a wise Majapa. No evil can come from bringing him to the Yahi World.*

So, taking only what they would need for the night, the three of them slid and crawled down the steep canyon side, through manzanita and chaparral and poison oak, coming out on Banya Creek at Gahma. Flat, free of brush, carpeted with green clover, deep water flowed quietly against the crescent-moon bow of land.

"Now I see why the Yahi called Gahma the Dambusa Village," said Majapa.

Ishi made fire with his firedrill, choosing a place below the old houses. He put rocks from the creek into the fire to heat. As the fire burned down, he and Majapa and Maliwal built a rough shelter over it. "This is no proper watgurwa, but it will do," he said. Then the three of them lay down, inside the shelter. Not since the day he left the Yahi World had Ishi felt the deep nothingness of the watgurwa sweatbath, and Maliwal and Majapa had never known it until now.

Ishi roused himself and sang the old ritual songs and recited the Ending Prayer. The hair and faces and naked bodies of the bathers were streaming with sweat; sweat dripped from their shoulders and the ends of their noses. They slipped into the quiet water off Gahma and swam upstream and back downstream. Then they sat on the bank while Ishi lighted a pipe of sacred tobacco, and blew smoke to the Sky World, to the Underneath World, and to the North and West and East and South—the Earth Directions. He gave Majapa and Maliwal powdered tobacco to blow from their flat open palms while he recited the Purification Prayer.

"Aiku tsub! It is well begun. Now we go down the creek." They went below the alder log. Ishi motioned the others to wait for him while he went alone to the place where he had found the Little One's shells.

It is as when I was last here.

He came back and crossed the alder log to the fishing shelter. It was as he last saw it, purified, empty. He called to Majapa, "Come, we fish!" Barefoot, Majapa and Maliwal ran across the slippery log.

Ishi took Maliwal where he could cast for salmon from the bank. He and Majapa swam to the rock in the middle of the creek. "It is my old fishing place," said Ishi. "I want you to take the first salmon here."

Salmon were swimming swiftly upstream against the current. Majapa made a good throw, harpooning one of the sacred fish of the springtime and the New Year, a salmon with gleaming scales like moonlight.

"Aiku tsub! The sacred fish comes to you! The Spirits are not angry or fearful to have you here!"

Leaving the harpoon to Majapa, Ishi went into the creek, where the water was swift and deep, to catch the fish of the New Year in the old way, in his bare hands; to swim once again as salmon swims, powerfully, upstream.

Later, they broiled their catch on sticks, the fat dripping into the fire zzzzzs, zzzzzs. As they ate, they put the bones on leaves to dry before the fire, to be ground and eaten later, that they might have some of salmon's strength.

They sat around the fire, saying little, Ishi and Majapa smoking. When a log was added, Maliwal pulled the drying salmon bones away from the freshened blaze. In the dusk, bats and swallows swept the air noiselessly, hunting. The full moon of the New Year rose over Waganupa, making the canyon a patchwork of flat blacks and whites.

There was the restlessness of four-footers which comes with the full moon; of twigs snapping in the brush; of an unseen secret race through the trees. Buzzards roosted in the upper branches of a dead gray pine; they kept changing roosting places long after they were usually asleep. There was chattering among the smaller birds, and a nestful of yellowhammer woodpeckers waked and cried yagka yakga!

From the canyon rose a lonesome chorus of doves, owls, toads and frogs. Majapa and Maliwal lay down by the fire and slept. Ishi was wide awake, listening. The bright night was like the night he carried his friend down Banya Canyon; it was like the night he sat awake beside Mother, staring down into the darkness, wondering if the Lost Ones were safe in the fishing shelter across the creek.

He started up: he knew what he must do. In the moonlight he moved more swiftly than in daylight. Sometimes he slipped, and scratched and bruised himself on thorny bushes and sharp rocks, invisible in the blackness of the shadows. Running, he went on and so came to Ancestor Cave. Inside the cave he prayed and burned tobacco on the flat stone slab under which the Ancestors lay. The bright moon of spring had dipped below the edge of the earth before Ishi came out of the cave, but he came with a peaceful heart.

It seemed to me my father's Spirit breathed on me in the cave, letting me know all is well, that I should shoot the arrows which I made in the museum-watgurwa; that I should hunt the deer once again.

Ishi was back in Gahma before Sun reached the sleeping ones and wakened them.

Ishi, Majapa, and Maliwal built at Gahma a summer shelter with a canopy of maple branches and leaves to give a light shade. They dug a firepit where they cooked, and their food was deer, salmon, trout, quail, brodiaea bulbs, young greens, early cherries and plums.

Going barefoot, Majapa and Maliwal moved

over the green hills and through the brush almost as silently as Ishi. Their voices, too, became more like Ishi's, closer to the soft brush-voice of the People. The hunted with the bow, and fished with the harpoon and the net. They took a sweatbath each day, and swam in the deep pool beside Gahma. They lay under the brilliant starts at night while Ishi told what he remembered of Grandmother's tales of the Star People; or Majapa told some of the Star stories of other Peoples. They sang Yahi songs and Maliwal learned to dance with Ishi the Dance of the Young Hunter.

Said Ishi one night, "We make a larger fire than my People ever made in my memory. They did not dare let the flames leap up and repeat themselves upside down in the water. It would have told the saldu where they were." Then he laughed. "It is strange to say the 'saldu' in this old way—the saldu, the enemy. The saldu—my friends!"

Said Majapa, "You once were afraid you would change into a saldu. Do you think if Maliwal and I lived here during a turning of the four seasons we would cease to be whitemen?"

Ishi studied his friends before answering. "Su! You, Majapa, already smoke the stone pipe and have learned much wisdom. Your skin and that of the wanasi becomes the color of madrone bark under the canyon Sun. The wanasi shoots the bow as I shot it when I reached only as far as the ornament in Elder Uncle's nose, which is as close to the Sky as Maliwal has grown.

"But—there must be no hair on the face of the Majapa. Each day you will have to pull out those hairs which grow during the night. And the hair of the head must grow long. As for this Young Wolf, I think we must use pitch on his no-color hair, else he will be as a white deer among a herd of brown ones."

Ishi and Maliwal played the Meadow Game; they climbed bare, vertical cliffs, using a rope; and they jumped down over bluffs into heavily leaved trees, sliding safely to the ground as Ishi and the Restless One used to do. Maliwal became a swimmer able to go underwater for long distances. Sometimes when the strength of the current was too much for him, he held onto Ishi's brush of hair as the Little One once did.

Maliwal did not always go with the other two, preferring to hunt alone for a day, or to go into the higher hills with no purpose but to dream. "It is the age to begin to dream," said Ishi, letting him go. *Young Wolf can take care of himself. Perhaps a Power Dream will come to him.*

Together, Ishi and Majapa repeated the journey Ishi took when he was young, and they went even beyond that journey, beyond Upper Meadow and Bushki to the cave of the White Dream, on to the top of Waganupa, and down to the bottom of the gorge of Yuna Canyon. They traveled up and down the lowlands and the uplands of the Yahi World and at the end they went again to Wowunupo.

THE MOON of the New Year had come and gone and another moon was full since the three left the museum-watgurwa. Ishi sat beside Banya Creek at Gahma, beside the stream of home. High on the ledge above him, hidden, was Wowunupo. Downstream was the shelter where he and Mother spent their last moons together. Ishi sat alone, thinking of his mother and the Little One and his uncle.

Aii—ya! Once again I sit by this stream and dream of all that was and is no more.

Late afternoon shadows stretched across the creek. Majapa came quietly after a while and sat beside Ishi. Ishi filled his pipe and passed the pouch of tobacco to Majapa. They smoked in silence while Banya Creek flowed on, toward the Daha and Outer Ocean. Majapa skipped a flat pebble smoothly across the water. Ishi smiled.

"Here are the notebooks," said Majapa after the smoke was finished, the pipes knocked out and put back in their pouches.

One book was full of Yahi talk. "We say these words so many times, back and forth, I know what this writing means." Ishi leafed through the notebook, murmuring some of the words that were written there.

Another notebook named the plants the Yahi used, and the Yahi four-footers and birds and fish. There were three notebooks of map pictures. Ishi looked at them one by one. His and Majapa's journeys up and down Yuna and Banya Canyons and to Waganupa were marked on a map, and the hills and ridges, the creeks, gorges, waterfalls, and the caves and meadows of the Yahi World were on another. Still others showed where were the stream crossings; where fish weirs were built; where acorns were picked, and ferns and grasses; where juniper wood was cut and wood for the sacred fires in the watgurwa. And there were maps which showed the villages where Ishi lived and the old villages where the People lived in the time before the coming of the saldu; where they buried their dead, where they danced and feasted and hunted.

Ishi closed the last notebook. Said Majapa, "So much is done. Not all, but some of the Way is here." He patted the notebooks. "Does it seem good to you?"

"Good, good." Ishi smiled at his friend. "We are like Kaltsuna and Jupka, you and I. We sit on Waganupa and say where the villages are, and how the hunting is done, and what the People speak."

"Shall we become a little lizard and a butterfly?"

"M'm'h—su. If so, I shall be Lizard, a maker of arrows, and you, Butterfly, a maker of words."

There was another long silence before Majapa said, "I must return to the museum-watgurwa. I wondered, seeing you sitting here by the stream of home, whether you wished to stay?"

Ishi shook his head. "No, I do not wish to stay. . . . Long ago I said to you this is a dead world; you said it was not dead, that you and I remembered it. I was not sure then of your meaning. . . . But it is dead here." Ishi waved his arm toward Waganupa and the hills. "Only the dead bones of dead Yahi are here. The People are in the Land of the Dead, and in the notebooks.

"It is with you I speak the Tongue. Your dream and mine and the Little Lost One's meet at the Edge of the World which is part saldu and part Yahi.

"Sitting here in Gahma, I am thinking of the museum-watgurwa, of my workplace. There are many things I have not yet made for the Yahi room, and many matters you have not yet written in the notebooks."

"The notebooks fill fast here, O Elder Brother of Maliwal," Majapa was partly teasing, partly serious. "And I am going to miss Gahma."

"Aii! You will miss Gahma. You too! And Maliwal will miss Gahma. Let us say we will return when we can, the three of us?"

"Aiku tsub!"

Majapa and Ishi talked late that night by their last fire. Said Majapa, "We speak here of the Old Ways, of the Olden Days. But, tell me, my friend, what do you make of the saldu World, now that you are again, for the space of two moons, in your old World?"

Ishi took a stick with which he stirred the ashes at the edge of the fire, making a map picture in the ashes as he had done on the notebook paper. At last he dropped the stick into the fire, and rubbed a foot over the ashes picture. "Your question is not to be answered in a word. . . . There are many saldu—too many I sometimes say to myself when I see them crowding each other in the streets and hear their harsh voices, speaking too loud and quarreling as they do.

"There are many kinds of saldu. There are those like you and Maliwal and the Kuwi and my other friends—to them I feel as to Elder Uncle, to the Restless One, to my People.

"The saldu Gods and the saldu Heroes are beyond the understanding of a Yahi. They are clever, much cleverer than Jupka and Kaltsuna and the Yahi Heroes. They give their People wheels, quick-fire, and the strong iron and steel for making tools; they give them many, many good things. . . . But it seems to me they do not much care that their People should be wise. They seem not to have set a Way—a clear Way —for the saldu to follow.

"This is why, even if I wished to stay in Gahma, I must return to the museum-watgurwa. Elder Brother must stay near to Young Wolf. The wanasi is clear about the Way now. He follows it. It is my wish he shall not lose or forget it; not be drawn into trouble and confusion by those who are themselves troubled and confused.

"And—you, Majapa—my heart is not easy for you. If the evil of war comes, I wish to be close to Outer Ocean until that evil passes. I will quiet the waves with acorn meal, and the smoke of the sacred tobacco will go on the air to you and curl around you.

"When you are back from that war, we will

207

work, you and I. And we will come again to Gahma, for a little.

"For the rest, I will grow old in the museum-watgurwa. It is there, with my friends, I will die."

ISHI lived for many moons, a museum man among museum men. Death came to him as he wished—with his friends in the museum-watgurwa. Majapa and the museum men released his Spirit in the old Yahi way. And they saw to it that Ishi had with him those things a Yahi hunter must take from the World of the Living, for the journey to the west: his own best bow and five good arrows; a small basket of acorn meal, enough for five days; and his treasure bundle.

In the bundle were the scrap of Mother's hat from Wowunupo, the shells from Tushi's necklace which Ishi had found on the bank of Banya Creek, the shells he had picked up at the Edge of the World, and a few pieces of his favorite rock-glass. In his belt was his stone pipe and his pouch filled with sacred tobacco.

For five days Majapa and Maliwal went at sundown to Outer Ocean. There, at the Edge of the World, they cried for their friend and scattered acorn meal on the waves and said a prayer. But there was no end to Maliwal's tears and Majapa saw that he must help him. He recalled to Maliwal Ishi's words: "It is a five day's journey down the Spirit Trail, and at its end is the Yahi Land of the Dead, where the Old Ones, the Ancestors, live. Tushi will meet me there and take me to the firepit of my family. Grandfather and Grandmother will be there, and Elder Uncle and my mother and my father. I will never again be separated from Tushi and my father."

It seemed to Maliwal that it was Ishi himself beside him, speaking in his soft brush voice. He dried his tears, and with Majapa, turned away from the ocean. Together they walked back up the wet sand shore. Sun was underneath the earth, on his way to the east and another day's journey over the top of the Sky. The sand was no longer wet underfoot. They came to the edge of the park. There, above the treetops, a new moon of spring shone like a Yahi bow at full draw.

AUTHOR'S NOTE

ISHI, LAST OF HIS TRIBE is a story from history. Ishi was an American Indian born in 1861 or 1862. His tribe was the Yana, and his parents belonged to the southernmost of the Yana who called themselves the Yahi.

The Yana lived in the western foothills of Mount Lassen, in northern California. They were old on the land, their ancestors having lived there for three or four thousand years or more. The land belonged to no one before them; they were its first native sons.

The gold rush to California brought the first Europeans or white men into Yana country, twelve years before Ishi was born. By the time he was ten years old, the Yana had been killed or driven from their homes by the white invaders. Only the young boy Ishi and a handful of other Yahi were left. Unknown to the white men, they hid in the canyons of Mill and Deer Creeks, living on as best they could in the old Yahi way.

It was in 1908 that the work crew of a power company discovered their village; and it was in 1911 that Ishi was found in the corral of a slaughterhouse outside Oroville, the last survivor of his people.

Ishi's "museum-watgurwa" is the Museum of Anthropology of the University of California; it was then situated on Parnassus Heights in San Francisco, next to the Medical School. There, Ishi died in March, 1916.

Ishi lived long enough to leave a record of what the Yana were like. White men now know how Ishi's people lived; who were some of their

Gods and Heroes; what was their language, in ordinary speech and in story and song; and something of Yahi courage and conduct and manners and the Yahi Way of Life. This book tries to look back on Ishi's life, on the old Yahi World, and the world of the white man as seen through Ishi's eyes.

àiku tsub / it is well; it is good
àizuna / your own; my own
auna / fire
banya / deer
daana / baby
Daha / large river; the Sacramento
dambusa / pretty, gentle
dawana / crazy, wild
hàxa / yes
hèxai-sa! / go away!
hildàga / star
hìsi, ìshi / man
Jùpka / name of a God; butterfly
Kaltsùna / name of a God; lizard
kùwi / doctor
mahdè / sick
majàpa / headman
maliwàl / wolf
marìmi / woman
Mechi-Kùwi / Demon Doctor
moocha / tobacco
nizè ah Yàhi / I am of the People
sàldu / white man; white men
sigàga / quail
sìwini / pine wood
su! / so! ah! well!
suwa! / thus it is!
Tèhna-Ishi / Bearcub Boy
tètna / bear
Waganùpa / Mount Lassen
wakàra / full moon
wanàsi / young hunter;
hunters

watgùrwa / men's house
wòwi / family house
Wowùnupo–mu–tètna / grizzly
bear's hiding place
Yàhi / the People
yùna / acorn

ABOUT THE AUTHOR

THEODORA KROEBER was born in Denver, Colorado, and lived her first seventeen years in Telluride, a mining camp in the Rocky Mountains. Across the range, a day's horseback ride from Telluride, was another mining camp, Ouray, named for the Ute Indian, Chief Ouray. Mrs. Kroeber says, "My brothers and I took Indians pretty much for granted. Our horses came from Ute Indians who trained them to take the steep trails at an easy gait which did not jolt and tire horse or rider. We rode on horseback to visit various cliff dwellings before the road was put into Mesa Verde Park; and the floors of our home were covered with rugs from the looms of Navajo women who wove them."

Mrs. Kroeber's husband, Alfred Kroeber, was Chairman of the Department of Anthropology and Curator of the Museum of Anthropology and Ethnology of the University of California when Ishi was discovered in 1911. He and Ishi became close friends. Professor and Mrs. Kroeber and their four children came to know many Indians, some of whom visited the Kroebers in their home in Berkeley.

These Indians worked with Mr. Kroeber, dictating to him the words of their language, and telling him the Way of Life of their people. Many returned year after year to spend some weeks—perhaps their vacation—with the Kroebers. When work for the day was done, then children and grown-ups played shinny in the old Indian way; or they practiced shooting the bow; or they went swimming; or played croquet. And in the evening, they sat around the fire and talked and told stories. Sometimes they sang songs and danced an Indian dance to the accompaniment of a gourd rattle.

Theodora Kroeber is the author of *The Inland Whale*, a collection of California Indian tales, and *Ishi In Two Worlds*, an anthropological study of Ishi's life and times. Mrs. Kroeber says, "When I write, I turn most often to something Indian. This is not because I am an Indian 'specialist,' or feel that I have anything novel to say about Indians, but because I find their stories beautiful and true and their way of telling a story to be also my way."

ABOUT THE ILLUSTRATOR

RUTH ROBBINS is a designer and illustrator of many books. She is also the author of *Baboushka and the Three Kings*, for which she won the Caldecott Medal Award in 1961, and *The Emperor and the Drummer Boy*.

Before creating the drawings in the text of *ISHI*, she made a trip into the Yahi country where Ishi and his tribe lived, and where much of the land remains in its natural state of steep ridges, rocky gorges and lively flowing streams.

TEENAGERS FACE LIFE AND LOVE

Choose books filled with fun and adventure, discovery and disenchantment, failure and conquest, triumph and tragedy, life and love.

☐	13359	**THE LATE GREAT ME** Sandra Scoppettone	$1.95
☐	13691	**HOME BEFORE DARK** Sue Ellen Bridgers	$1.75
☐	13671	**ALL TOGETHER NOW** Sue Ellen Bridgers	$1.95
☐	14836	**PARDON ME, YOU'RE STEPPING ON MY EYEBALL!** Paul Zindel	$2.25
☐	11091	**A HOUSE FOR JONNIE O.** Blossom Elfman	$1.95
☐	14306	**ONE FAT SUMMER** Robert Lipsyte	$1.95
☐	14690	**THE CONTENDER** Robert Lipsyte	$2.25
☐	13315	**CHLORIS AND THE WEIRDOS** Linn Platt	$1.95
☐	12577	**GENTLEHANDS** M. E. Kerr	$1.95
☐	12650	**QUEEN OF HEARTS** Bill & Vera Cleaver	$1.75
☐	12741	**MY DARLING, MY HAMBURGER** Paul Zindel	$1.95
☐	13555	**HEY DOLLFACE** Deborah Hautzig	$1.75
☐	13897	**WHERE THE RED FERN GROWS** Wilson Rawls	$2.25
☐	20170	**CONFESSIONS OF A TEENAGE BABOON** Paul Zindel	$2.25
☐	14730	**OUT OF LOVE** Hilma Wolitzer	$1.75
☐	14225	**SOMETHING FOR JOEY** Richard E. Peck	$2.25
☐	14687	**SUMMER OF MY GERMAN SOLDIER** Bette Greene	$2.25
☐	13693	**WINNING** Robin Brancato	$1.95

Buy them at your local bookstore or use this handy coupon for ordering:

Bantam Books, Inc., Dept. EDN, 414 East Golf Road, Des Plaines, Ill. 60016

Please send me the books I have checked above. I am enclosing $_____ (please add $1.00 to cover postage and handling). Send check or money order —no cash or C.O.D.'s please.

Mr/Mrs/Miss _____

Address _____

City _____ State/Zip _____

EDN—7/81

Please allow four to six weeks for delivery. This offer expires 1/82.

READ THE BOOKS THAT MAKE A DIFFERENCE

Fiction and non-fiction, here are the books that tell the stories of America's minority groups—personal stories, documented accounts, past and present experiences. They affect us all—don't miss them.

☐	13529	**FAREWELL TO MANZANAR** Jeanne Wakatsuki Houston & James D. Houston	$1.95
☐	13597	**BURY MY HEART AT WOUNDED KNEE** Dee Brown	$3.50
☐	14978	**THE INDIAN HERITAGE OF AMERICA** Alvin M. Josephy, Jr.	$3.95
☐	20316	**THE BLACK POETS** Dudley Randall, ed.	$3.50
☐	20508	**ISHI, LAST OF HIS TRIBE** Theodore Kroeber	$2.50
☐	13904	**I KNOW WHY THE CAGED BIRD SINGS** Maya Angelou	$2.50
☐	14470	**GATHER TOGETHER IN MY NAME** Maya Angelou	$2.50
☐	13307	**FOR COLORED GIRLS WHO HAVE CONSIDERED SUICIDE/WHEN THE RAINBOW IS ENUF** Ntozake Shange	$2.50
☐	13113	**NAPPY EDGES** Ntozake Shange	$2.50